P9-EJU-733

THRICE TOLD TALES

also by CATHERINE LEWIS

Postcards to Father Abraham

Dry Fire

THRICE TOLD TALES

CATHERINE LEWIS

illustrated by Joost Swarte

ATHENEUM BOOKS FOR YOUNG READERS
New York London Toronto Sydney New Delhi

atheneum

ATHENEUM BOOKS FOR YOUNG READERS

An imprint of Simon & Schuster Children's Publishing Division

1230 Avenue of the Americas, New York, New York 10020

ATHENEUM BOOKS FOR YOUNG READERS is a registered
trademark of Simon & Schuster, Inc.

Atheneum logo is a trademark of Simon & Schuster, Inc.

For information about special discounts for bulk purchases,
please contact Simon & Schuster Special Sales at 1-866-506-1949
or business@simonandschuster.com.

The Simon & Schuster Speakers Bureau can bring authors to
your live event. For more information or to book an event, contact
the Simon & Schuster Speakers Bureau at 1-866-248-3049 or visit
our website at www.simonspeakers.com.

Book design by Debra Sfetsios-Conover

The text for this book is set in Archer.

The illustrations for this book are rendered in ink.

Manufactured in the United States of America

First Edition

10 9 8 7 6 5 4 3 2

Library of Congress Cataloging-in-Publication Data

Lewis, Catherine.

Thrice told tales / Catherine Lewis. — 1st ed.

p. cm.

ISBN 978-1-4169-5784-3

ISBN 978-1-4424-6076-8 (eBook)

1. Literature—Terminology. 2. Authorship—Juvenile literature.

I. Title.

PN44.5.L438 2013

803—dc23   2012010644

To all MUS in captivity. May your days of suffering
soon come to an end.
—C. L.

To my youngest daughter, Loulou
—J. S.

CONTENTS

STORY

Three blind mice ran after the farmer's wife.
She cut off their tails with a carving knife.

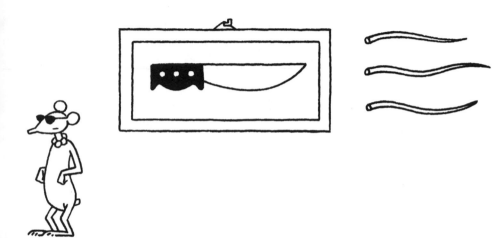

Snip of the Tale: On the most basic level, a sequence of events.

PLOT

Three blind mice ran after the farmer's wife. She cut off their tails with a carving knife because

she

was

a

SADIST.

Snip of the Tale: What happens and why.

METAFICTION

Three blind mice are running after the farmer's wife to seek revenge for what she did to their tails—she cut them off, as we already know. Or so that's what we assume from what we've been told. Actually, that's not the whole story. You see, our three tailless friends were foraging along the bathroom windowsill for dead flies and came across the wife's facial cream. There, stamped on the edge of the tube, was the pernicious batch number 1476203, a number that, in spite of its length, was engraved in the brain of each mouse. Why? you might ask. Because this batch contained a large dose of alpha hydroxy acid, which killed their fourteen siblings. *Squirt, squirt, squirt,* right into their eyes. Although the three we are now following were subjected to the same treatment, they survived, at first completely blinded. But thanks to their quick thinking and access to clean water, which they used to rinse their red eyes, they regained partial sight. (How could they possibly chase after the farmer's wife if they were 100 percent blind?) I am happy to report that our three rodents' eyes continue to heal, though very slowly, thus allowing for the events that I've chronicled in the following pages.

Snip of the Tale: Fiction that comments on itself.

THE LENSES OF PSYCHIC DISTANCE

Telescope
Three rodents, members of the species *Mus musculus*, known among other things for their capacity to carry diseases such as the deadly hantavirus, were attempting to invade the Bethoon farmhouse.

Binoculars
The mice stood on top of the hill and looked at the farmhouse, wondering how they would get inside.

Magnifying Glass
Pee Wee saw the farmhouse and started to run. Ouch. His blister hurt, he hoped it wasn't getting infected. Mary pulled him back by the tail. The farm seemed ideal, almost too perfect. She turned to Oscar, who was standing on his hind legs and sniffing the air. He wondered if the farmer had a daughter and if those stories were really true. "Smells okay to me," he said. Pee Wee trotted down the hill. After him, Oscar, then Mary, who whispered to herself, "Oh please."

Snip of the Tale: By choosing to write from outside or from inside a character, an author can influence how involved the reader feels with the character.

IMMEDIACY

"Aaaargh," squeals Pee Wee, "my tail! My tail!" He stands there holding his bloody stub between his paws. The other two scurry over for closer inspection. What could be worse than that?

Snip of the Tale: Often unfolds as a scene in the present tense and uses the character's own words. As a result, the reader feels she is right there when things are happening.

IRONY
IN YOUR FACE OR NOT. YOU FOOL.

Sarcasm

Mary insisted that Oscar go with them to the meeting. Pee Wee begged him to come along too. Soon he found himself sitting in a circle of strangers. Oy. The counselor at Survivors Anonymous spoke first. "Oscar, tell us how you feel about losing your tail."

"Elated. That's right. I was hoping someone would cut off my tail because with a tail I couldn't come here and hang out with all you winners."

Subtlety

Mary had spent the entire night foraging for food and had found only a small crust of bread. It wouldn't be enough to feed the three of them. She thought of the nutritious pellets spilling out of the feed trough in her cage at Love Your Face Laboratory, Inc.

Mary had dreamed of the things she would do as a free mouse. She rubbed her blistered paw. Funny, she hadn't imagined this.

Ignorance

Pee Wee was thrilled to find a sugar cube. Wow, food for two days. He dragged it across the room and shoved it into the water drain for storage.

Snip of the Tale: Saying the opposite of what one means is perhaps the most obvious form of irony, but there are subtler forms at work in fiction, such as when a character doesn't get precisely what she hoped for, but something less clear-cut. There can be irony in ignorance, too, when readers know something the character doesn't.

RED HERRING

Oscar yawned. "So whose turn is it?" The heat under the refrigerator was making him groggy.

"It's Pee Wee's," said Mary, "but I really don't like sending him out there alone."

Oscar lassoed his tail around a refrigeration coil and hung upside down like a bat. "Why don't we all go? I could use some fresh air and exercise."

"Can we? Can we? That'll be such fun."

Oscar raised his lips and smirked. "Fun for us, not the farmer's wife."

They filed out from under the refrigerator with Oscar in the lead. He came to a dead stop. Pee Wee and Mary stumbled into him.

"It's the cat," he whispered.

"C-c-cat?" Pee Wee shivered.

The cat was enormous, truly gargantuan. He was sitting on his ample hindquarters, cleaning his front paws, his yellow eyes half closed. He sat there leisurely licking his fur, and the wet sandpaper of his tongue sounded as if he were cleaning and sharpening his whole body all at the same time. His claws came out. They hooked the air like raised scimitars. Then he sauntered out of the room.

"Now!" cried Oscar. Without looking back, he led the charge. "Aim for the right ankle!"

With a howl of disgust, the farmer's wife seized a large knife from the counter and turned to face her attackers.

Snip of the Tale: Much ado about nothing in relation to the story. (Despite the cat's menacing description, the cat was neither violent nor central to the story.) Red herrings can be related to characters, plots, and cheap tricks that mislead.

SUSPENSION OF DISBELIEF

Three blind mice sat around an old wooden spool of thread playing cards. Mary flicked what was left of her tail impatiently. "Come on!"

Pee Wee leaned forward and studied his cards. A pair of kings, not bad. He put two Cheerios on the table and squinted in Oscar's direction.

The air was clouded with smoke. Oscar had raided the people's ashtray from the night before. He stubbed out the butt in a bottle cap and upped the ante by a peanut.

"You're bluffing," said Mary.

"Yeah, like last week when I said, 'Knife, run for your life.'"

Snip of the Tale: This occurs when the reader willingly accepts improbabilities in fiction and therefore is able to go with the flow of the story. Notice that everything the mice do in this book requires a suspension of disbelief.

NAMES

Once upon a time there were three blind mice named Oscar, Omar, and Oman.

Noooo way. Scratch.

Once upon a time there were three blind mice named Mary Puresnow, Robert Allgood, and James Mosttempted.

Absurd. Scratch that, too.

Once upon a time there were three blind mice named Larry, Curly, and Moe.

No, you stooge.

Once upon a time there were three blind mice named Rainbow Farnsworth III, Seymour Butts, and Purple Hayes.

Oy. Scratch.

Oh, for Pete's sake. Once upon a time there were three blind mice, surname: Mouse. First names: Pee Wee, Mary, and Oscar.

Snip of the Tale: The sound and length of names, along with their associations, all play a role in giving life to characters, often by suggesting something about their identity.

LEITMOTIF

Matilda Bethoon chop/chop/chops/ slender parsnips. She wields her Ginsu knife with precision, a steal at $19.95. It's razor sharp, but neither it nor other kitchen toys—bamboo steamer, Teflon spoons—can assuage her agitation. She clenches a bunch of carrots and whacks off their green tops. *Chop. Chopchop. Chopchopchop.* An orange chip slaps the floor. Matilda stoops to pick it up. Yikes! Three mice charge her, trailing their dirty wigglers. "Hiyah." ///

Snip of the Tale: Something that reoccurs in a work (an image, object, action, word, phrase, etc.) that tends to unify the work and establish a theme.

AVANT-GARDE

Wee Pee named mice blind three were there time a upon Once ⟵
Oscar, and Mary who mastered the serendipitous maze and managed
free, Once. experimentation laboratory further of fate the escape to
they ran.

 They ran, ran, ran.
 Pee Wee ran.
 Mary ran.
 Oscar ran.

$$\overset{o}{N} \qquad \overset{o}{h}\ p \qquad \overset{o}{h}\ p \qquad \overset{o}{h}\ p\ \overset{p}{i}\ \overset{n}{g}$$ was allowed.

𝒮nip of the Tale: **Writing that challenges
(or even attacks) the traditional forms or
ideas of art.**

CAUSE AND EFFECT

Three mice become legally blind when scientists at Love Your Face Laboratory Inc., squirt copious amounts of alpha hydroxy acid into their eyes. As a result of this torture, the trio plans an escape for themselves and all the other critters. Once free, they retaliate by chewing the coating off of a 220-volt line. They cross the stripped wires and drop them into a petri dish containing a chemical accelerant. A fire burns the research lab to the ground. Three months later Love Your Face Laboratory, Inc., files for bankruptcy. Insurance investigators cite arson and fail to pay the insured party. Satisfied that the mad scientists have been put out of business, the mice head to the country for a much-needed vacation.

Snip of the Tale: A pebble thrown into the water creates a series of rings. In the same way, any occurrence will have consequences, which may lead to other occurrences. This interlinking gives structure to a story and helps to make it believable.

STREAM OF **CONSCIOUSNESS**

Licorice jelly bean, shiny and black! Want it. Want it. Want it. Don't have one in my treasure. Got dimes. Shiny dimes. Got paper clips. Safety pins. What else? Charm bracelet—Eiffel Tower, horse, pistol-bang-bang-you're-dead, Scottie dog, hourglass, megaphone—love that charm bracelet. Got foil ball. Got silver dollar. Two jacks. Got nickels. Quarters. Half-dollars. Mirror. Monopoly hat—Oscar will be mad when he can't find that. What else, what else? No shiny jelly bean, that's for sure. Oh, and it smells so good. What to do. What to do.

Snip of the Tale:
Writing that attempts to go deep into the character's brain, where thoughts are often fragmented—peppered with images, past experiences, dreams, etc.

THE GARDEN STATE'S ONE-HUNDRED-FOOT MOUSE

In the 1800s a Hoboken farmer plowed up what he thought was barbed wire. He laid down his plow to investigate. The thing spun from his hands. "That varmint weren't no barbed wire."

Three weeks later a woman picking snap peas in her garden saw a tail slithering. She grabbed it and declared, "Why, it's a brown field mouse with an enormous tail." It squeaked in fear and bit her finger.

News quickly spread of the one-hundred-foot tailed mouse that could choke a man to death like an anaconda.

"That is, if he don't bite you first."

"Heard he took the hand of a woman clean off while she was picking peas."

"Best to give 'im something he likes and maybe he'll leave us alone."

Today it has come to pass that every year at first planting in Hoboken the residents leave a jar of assorted nuts in their garden, while the more cautious residents always make sure to wear shoes and gloves as well.

Snip of the Tale: A story handed down that is unverifiable but not impossible.

V O C A B U L A R Y

Trinity of myopic vermin
Eyeless murine trio
Triumvirate of sightless rodents
Three blind mice

Behold them scud!
To what extent they make haste—observe!
Notice whereby they bolt!
See how they run!

Pee Wee, Oscar, and Mary chased Matilda.
Ms. Bethoon was pursued by the mice.
Each and every one of them made after the wife of the agriculturalist.
They all ran after the farmer's wife.

Matilda hacked off the rear appendages of Pee Wee, Oscar, and Mary with a knife.

With a stainless steel blade the farmer's wife cut the hinder part of the voles.

This time she used a mandolin and julienne-sliced their carrot-shaped caudae.

She cut off their tails with a carving knife.

Can you recall an incident like the one described above?
Is this an anomaly or what?
Did you ever see such a thing in your life,
As three blind mice?

Snip of the Tale: The choice of individual words (vocabulary) and the way they're arranged (syntax) influence the reading experience. See "Diction."

SHOWING AND TELLING

Show
Oscar's paw slipped off the window ledge. He counterflipped his tail. What tail? "Oh NOOOooooooooo!" *Thump*.

Tell
Oscar missed his tail.

Show-and-Tell
"Look out!" Oscar fell off of the window ledge and thumped to the floor. Off balance again. Oh, for that enchanted rope of tail. He didn't have the courage to look at the frayed nub; instead he reached around and felt its coarse remainder, then shook his fist at the heavens. "Damn ye fates that shrink by half the tiniest creature."

Snip of the Tale: To show the reader something means that she can share in the experience more so than being told. Often, both are combined to tell a story.

DIALOGUE

Pee Wee huddled in a corner of the cage chewing on his paw. "We're never going to get out of here. Never. Never. Never."

"Oscar, let's tell him."

"No way. We don't even know if it's going to work."

Mary tugged on her necklace. "It'll work. It has to."

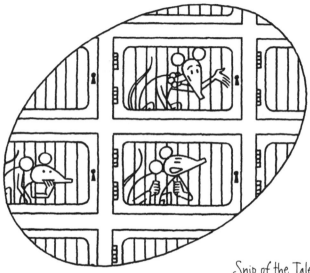

Snip of the Tale: Involves more than what is said. Most interesting when doing more than one thing at a time: revealing character, using gesture, advancing the story line, etc.

Mary sat on a box of matches, her legs dangling over the side, and rubbed her calloused paws against the strike plate. She had been on the run so long that her feet didn't feel like her own anymore. In the corner Pee Wee and Oscar dozed, their bodies outlined in a blanket of sheet music. The notes seemed to rise and fall as they breathed.

INTERIOR MONOLOGUE

Ouch. She looked at the dead skin that had accumulated beneath her—powdery and translucent—and rubbed more softly. In the sacristy she could hear the church mice preparing dinner. Were they ever going to eat? The church mice didn't have much food. Pasty wafers. A stagnant pool of drinking water by the door. Still, they seemed miraculously healthy. Tomorrow she and Oscar and Pee Wee would hit the road. She'd heard about a farmhouse with a big country kitchen. Her tail twitched at the delicious thought of biscuits and redeye gravy.

Snip of the Tale: Lets us know what the character is thinking.

SETTING

Underneath the refrigerator cool drops of water formed on the condensation coils. Oscar lapped up a mouthful, then slid into the drip pan to bathe. The Zen-like hum of the motor was so relaxing that in no time he was dreaming of apple pie with a warm slice of cheese on top. The farmer's wife had been baking, and the smell was heavenly.

"Oscar, wake up. Wake up, Oscar."

He opened an eye and saw Mary hunched over with worry. Not again. "This place is paradise, Mary. We're not leaving."

Mary's nose twitched. "Danger is everywhere." After what she'd had squirted in her eyes, she was especially afraid of the chemicals underneath the sink.

Oscar wiggled his toes in the water. "Pee Wee doesn't want to leave either."

"Pee Wee's too young to know what's best for him. He can hardly run, he's getting so chubby. She almost had him with the broom the other day."

Oscar ignored that comment. "He'll get depressed again if we move, do you want that? You see how he loves climbing inside of the toaster. It's his jungle gym. And the countertop is like a carnival. Cinnamon buns in the bread box, chocolate chips in the cookie jar, sugar cubes by the coffeepot." Oscar put his paw on her shoulder. "Mary, you're the only one who smells danger. I smell pie."

Snip of the Tale: When and where a story takes place.

SENTIMENTALITY

Big Cheese
Mouse Droppings Publisher, Inc.
Red Barn, North Dakota
US of A

Dear Pee Wee Mouse,
   As the last independent publisher of quality fiction specializing in mouse tragedies, we here at Mouse Droppings are interested in your manuscript. Unfortunately, we must refuse it in its present state due to sentimentality. Please review our remarks below, which will explain why *It's Such a Hard Life* is in need of revision.
   Your book contains stock situations (separation from a loved one, death, etc.), which can by themselves evoke strong feelings in a reader. You then attempt to manipulate the reader into a still more intense emotional reaction by lingering on these scenes. Passage in point:

   The cancerous lump in her belly had gotten so large that she could no longer crawl to the food trough. Why the White Coats injected her, no one knew, for never was there a kinder, sweeter mouse than Eva. The others gathered round, helplessly wringing their tails. "Don't be sad," Little Eva said. "Where I am going there are no more cages. But now I want to give each of you a whisker so that you'll always remember me until we meet again."

   We here at Mouse Droppings take fiction very seriously and want it to reflect the complexity and richness of life. This means we must engage the reader, but not hit her over the head with an emotion, telling her what to feel. Life is full of ambiguity, tension, and irony. That is what we hope to see in the fiction we publish. We would be happy to reconsider your manuscript were you to revise it in light of these comments.

Sincerely,
Big Cheese

$\int$nip of the Tale: When a writer simplifies and/or exaggerates the drama of a situation in order to provoke a strong feeling in the reader.

TITLE
SLIPPERY TO WHET

Pee Wee shuffled into the room and plunked down on a wine cork. "I'm stuck." He shoved the manuscript aside.

"Forget your story." Oscar bit into a pistachio nut, and shell fragments flew through the air. "What about *our* story? You could call it *Three Mice Blinded in a Laboratory Escape, Only to Have Their Tails Cut Off by a Farmer's Wife, but Saved Ultimately by Oscar the Magnificent.*"

"That's ridiculous," said Pee Wee. "Way too long and you give away the story. Plus, Oscar the Magnificent? Liar, liar, pants on fire."

Mary saw her two brothers were headed for a spat and interjected: "We've had a lot of adventures. How about *Tales Without End*?"

Shells flew across the room. "More like *End Without Tails.*"

"*Miceanthrope.*"

"*The Great Escape.*"

"*Of Mice and Meanies.*"

Mary said, "How about *Survival*? That's certainly one of our themes."

"What if we each told part of the story, then we could call it *Thrice Told Tales.*"

"That's a stupid idea and a stupid title."

Snip of the Tale: A billboard that advertises the writer's work, and yet something more. That something could be symbolic or metaphorical, contain a double meaning, reference another work, or be ironic or straightforward in its use of nouns.

MECHANICS
THREE BLIND LICE

Three blind lice
See how thay run
They all run after the farmers' wife
Who cut off there tales with a carving knife.
did you ever sea such a site in your life
As tree blind mice

Snip of the Tale: These basics include spelling, grammar, punctuation, and common sense—which all contribute to clarity.

TRANSITIONS
TIME, WHITE SPACE, AND DECLINE

Want to get from one place to the next in a story without getting lost? Forget GPS; subscribe to TTT Transitions, three for a dollar.

Time

Mary, Oscar, and Pee Wee ran after the farmer's wife. She cut off their tails with a carving knife. They all squealed and ran back underneath the refrigerator.

Forty-five minutes later all the bleeding had stopped. Only then did Pee Wee begin to cry, softly at first, like a dove's coo.

White Space

Once upon a time there were three blind mice named Mary, Oscar, and Pee Wee. They ran after Matilda Bethoon, the farmer's wife. She hacked off their tails with a carving knife.

Oscar yawned and wondered what he could eat for a snack; sadly, there weren't any dead flies left on the windowsill.

Decline

1. Oscar measured himself again. Had he really *shrunk a whole centimeter*? He sighed. He was aging, but he was still devilishly handsome.
2. By the time Mary finished her story, all the *marshmallows* in her mug *had melted*.

Snip of the Tale: These take the reader from one situation, place, or time to another. Transitions in and out of various points of view add to the possibilities.

FORESHADOWING
FORESHADOWING

"Pssssst. Over here." Mary was crouched on the kitchen counter. Pee Wee and Oscar ran to join her, but Pee Wee stopped when he passed the cookie jar. He could smell cookie.

"Come on." Oscar pulled Pee Wee's tail and got him moving again.

When they caught up to Mary, she pointed down into the sink with her paw. A large knife lay there, glinting in the moonlight that filtered through the kitchen window.

Oscar flicked his tail and then slid down the side of the sink until he was standing next to the knife. Tentatively he touched the blade with his paw. "Wow, that's sharp!"

Snip of the Tale: The use of an event, a character's thoughts, or a particular atmosphere to hint at what will happen later on.

Pee Wee's novel was chock-full of insertions. He found Oscar's Christmas list and included it:

Hey, Fat Red Man—bring me these things:
- Book of *1,001 Shakespearean Insults*
- A diamond-studded cape
  (no cubic zirconia)
- Magic wand
- Pistachios (Iranian, lime-cured, 5 lb.)
- *The Pyromaniac's Cookbook*, by O'Leary
- Matches (several boxes)

A transcript of Pee Wee's online chat with a crisis counselor:

Jim Dandy: State yr crisis
Pee Wee: Tail cut off w/ a knife
JD: how?
PW: me and O. and M. chased farmer's wife. She cut 'em all off.
JD: need ambulance?
PW: No, cut 2 mos. ago.
JD: 2 mos. ago! Why u calling now?
PW: What?
JD: You read me. 2 mos. ago—GET OVER IT ALREADY
PW: But I—
JD: yr 50 seconds R up. Need receipt for insurance?

Mary's nose turned red and twitched when she saw that Pee Wee—that dirty rat—had inserted an advertisement she had placed confidentially:

> **SWF with fine whiskers, dazzling red eyes, and slender nose seeks SM, sensitive and litter loving, to share romantic weekends. Cheese bingeing and people scaring a plus.**

There were even some pictures, like this before-and-after drawing of his tail:

Mary told Pee Wee he had gone too far when he inserted a book order just so he could play with the ISBN numbers:

The Psychology of Compulsive Eating: ISBN U84-6-2-7-Daze
How to Negotiate with the Opposite Sex: ISBN Y-U-1ook-5ooo-6E
The Jury's Verdict: ISBN URN4-15-2-1ife
Perils of Living in a Glass House: ISBN b.i.d.-ICUPP

𝒮nip of the Tale: As Oscar would say, these add a je ne sais quoi to the story. In addition to variety, something about character or situation is revealed in the above insertions.

ALLEGORY

"Who are you?" The gurgly voice was coming from a wet sponge lounging in a puddle of water in the kitchen sink.

"Me? I'm Knife," said the knife. "Who are you?"

The sponge squeezed herself to clear her vision. "I didn't recognize you through all the water. I'm Compassion."

"What are you doing here? You look worn out, ready for the garbage."

"Living here is exhausting. I wonder how the farmer can stand it? And his wife, Ms. Cruelty—trying to make her feel some pity for anything but herself is like banging your head against a wall."

"You don't have a head," Knife said pointedly.

"Don't be so literal." Compassion sighed and a few more droplets fell from her body. "And you, you're part of the problem. All your kind does is chop, chop, chop without asking why or what for."

"It's not my fault," said Knife. "I just do what I'm told."

"Hmmm." Compassion sat up and tried to erase the ring of scum around the sink. "I bet your real name is Mindless Indifference."

Snip of the Tale: A story where abstract ideas are dressed up as characters, objects, or settings in order to express and highlight ideas.

EPIGRAM

One for the novice; two for epigramphiles:

I.
On Common Sense

Never chase a woman with a knife
Especially if you're a mouse.

II.
On Immortality

A blind mouse with no tail,
The long tale of a white whale.

Snip of the Tale: A terse and witty quip often dealing with a single subject.

FAIRY TALE

Once upon a time three blind mice lived in a forest where they foraged for food. Their life was quite hard, for they had to compete with the birds for berries and the squirrels for nuts. Being blind compounded their difficulties. No sooner would they smell a ripe berry than a bird would land, pluck it, and fly off.

The first frost was chilling and the ground so hard that the mice didn't know what to do, for surely if they didn't freeze, they would become the food of owls and foxes. In the distance they could smell the warm smoke coming from the woodcutter's cabin, and after a brief discussion they decided to see if the woodcutter would let them stay the winter.

The woodcutter agreed, on the condition that they remain quietly in their nest during the day, as his wife was deathly afraid of mice. The woodcutter's wife often made mincemeat pie and at night the mice would come out and partake of it, especially the suet and apples, but during the day they remained out of sight, as promised, in their warm nest behind the stove.

By midwinter, however, the mice grew tired of sleeping all day and began to scurry inside the walls of the cabin. The woodcutter's wife heard the noise and said something to her husband that night. He assured her that it was only the sound of the crackling fire, but she remained nervous just the same. "I think we have mice."

"We don't have mice, and if we did, I'd fling them out into the cold."

The woodcutter's wife, knowing her husband to be the sort of man who couldn't say no even to a mouse, replied, "If you brought in mice, so help me, I'll cut off your nose with your own ax."

The mice overheard everything but paid no heed. Earlier and earlier they began to venture out into the cabin, until

at last, brazen as you please, they appeared in the daylight. One day around lunchtime the woodcutter's wife was making another mincemeat pie, scoring the top of the crust with her knife, when out of the corner of her eye she saw the mice and let loose a curdling scream that stunned them in their tracks. By the time they tried to run away, it was too late. The knife came down, *chop, chop, chop.*

Just then the woodcutter came into the cabin, where his wife, still in a rage, turned the knife toward him and cut off his nose. She then ran screaming from the cabin, never to be seen again. Surely the mice and the woodcutter would have bled to death had not a spark shot out of the stove and the tiniest of woodland fairies—no bigger than a fly—appeared. She tapped her tiny wand on the woodcutter's nose, and immediately it rose from the floor and reattached itself, as good as before.

"All the creatures of the forest know you are a kind and gentle man," said the fairy, and she promised him that before too long he would have a new wife equally as kind as himself.

The mice—who were in part to blame for all of this—evoked the fairy's pity, and she next turned her wand toward them. Although she did not restore each tail, she did restore their vision in its place, leaving them with hindsight and thus making them the shrewdest creatures in the forest. They kept their lovely nest (with full cabin amenities) and in exchange offered their wise counsel to the woodcutter on choosing a new wife. Soon the mice, the woodcutter, and his new bride were living happily ever after.

Snip of the Tale: Comes out of the folk tradition. Magic or supernatural elements are at work. Often something prohibited affects the plot.

FARCE
THE MICE MEET THE FAIRY GODMOTHER MISS VERONICA

So the tailless mice were standing there when a fairy god-mother appeared. She was wearing size 11 gold lamé pumps, a blue sequined cocktail dress, and a string of ruby beads that danced off of her Adam's apple when she said, "My, what have we here to-*day*?"

"That's just what I was about to ask," said Oscar.

She reached down and tickled Oscar's chin with her finger. "Oh honey, you are a live one even when your wire's down."

Oscar stamped his foot. "Just our luck."

"What do you mean?" asked Pee Wee. "I wished for a very odd mother just like you said."

"You wantwit, I said 'fairy godmother.'"

"Well, anyway, I think she's beautiful."

"Why, thank you, darlin'." Miss Veronica's glittering sequins caught the light and danced around her curves. Pee Wee wondered if he could gnaw off a strand of her dress without her knowing.

"Now, let's see if I can't get your tails back."

"I'd sooner have a sausage on my nose," said Oscar, "than let you touch my tail."

"As you wish." Miss Veronica opened a paper fan and fluttered it in the air.

"Get this sausage off my nose."

"But if she does," said Mary, "that uses a second wish, and then only one of us will get a tail."

Miss Veronica sang, "'Life is a cabaret, old chum,'" while the mice discussed their situation. They couldn't leave Oscar with a sausage on his nose and so wished it removed. Oscar felt his old schnoz return, then hastily said, "I wish you'd never come in the first place." Suddenly the mice were standing there with no tails. They blinked and looked around the room.

"Weird dream," said Oscar.

Pee Wee knew better. Over by the door he found a glittering blue strand of sequins. "Oh." He sighed. "Miss Veronica."

Snip of the Tale: Lowbrow comedy that aims for laughs and is known to use anything—puns, caricatures, sexual innuendos, and jokes—to elicit a hearty guffaw.

F _ _ K

It was snowing and the mice had nothing to do, so they sat around the table and wrote stories. Oscar asked Mary to read his and then got angry when she offered her opinion.

"Must you curse so much?"

"Hell yes. My characters can't talk without cursing."

Pee Wee looked up from his paper. "Mine can."

"Shut up." Oscar smacked him in the back of the head. "No one asked you."

"I'm not saying they shouldn't curse, just not so often," said Mary.

"Prude."

"Wonderful. You ask me to comment on your story and then insult me when I do. Who needs this?" Mary pushed back her chair.

"Don't leave, I'm . . ." Oscar rubbed his snout. Something muffled but vaguely resembling the word "sorry" came out.

Mary sat back down. "If cursing is a part of who they are, fine. But you've used the *F* word fourteen times on the first page. Shock has given birth to boredom."

"Yeah, it means about as much as the *F* word to a mailman."

"What?"

"Fragile."

Pee Wee had made a point and Oscar resisted the urge to slap him again.

"Cursing is a lot like dialect. You just need a little on the page and it goes a long way." Mary raised her finger. "Think about where your characters are when they curse and at whom. Cursing is not only about anger. I see you know that. Having your character talk dirty to her partner in the bedroom can be an intimate thing and tells us not only about her, but also about the relationship. But jeez, Oscar, every other word is an *F*, *S*, or *GD*. And I hate the *C* word."

Pee Wee's ears twitched. He looked up from his paper. "What's the *C* word?"

"Cooties. Go back to writing."

Snip of the Tale: Most readers don't mind an expletive or two if it's within character or if the situation merits it, but we become annoyed and bored to the point of abandoning the story when that's all we read. Conversely, we can smell prudish authors uncomfortable with topics like sex and the body and wish they would write about flowers instead.

interTEXTuality

"This place is paradise." Oscar yawned and folded his paws behind his head. He loved loafing underneath the fridge.

"Paradise? A farmhouse fraught with mousetraps?"

"I'm afraid of big, bad traps too," said Pee Wee.

Oscar sat up. "Okay, so no place is perfect, but this place is pretty darn close. I mean it. Imagine you could live anywhere. Where would it be?"

"Well," said Pee Wee, "if we lived in a house of straw, you could just roll over and chew. You could make lots of tunnels. I love the smell of fresh straw."

"It's not as strong as a house of sticks," said Mary. "With a house of sticks there's still plenty to chew on."

"Anyone could blow down a straw house," said Oscar, "and then where would you be?"

"I'd go live with Mary in her twig condo."

"Ha! Twigs burn faster than an albino mouse on the beach. What you need is a good old brick farmhouse just like the one we're in." With that, he inhaled, then dove into the drip pan, splashing Mary and Pee Wee.

Snip of the Tale: When one text references another work or works. Here there's reference to "The Three Little Pigs" and their housing dilemma in light of the Big Bad Wolf.

KEYBOARD DIGRESSION

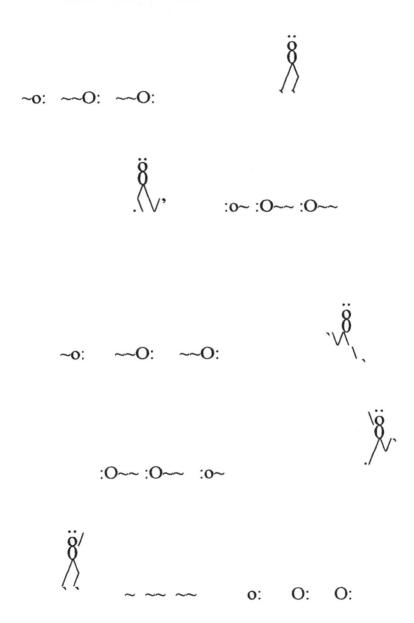

~o: ~~O: ~~O:

:o~ :O~~ :O~~

~o: ~~O: ~~O:

:O~~ :O~~ :o~

~ ~~ ~~   o: O: O:

Snip of the Tale: Even when they take a break, writers are still thinking about their work.

PICARO
THE ADVENTURES AND MISADVENTURES OF OSCAR D. MOUSE

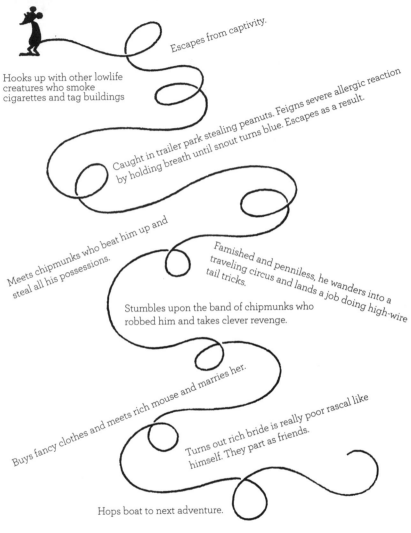

Escapes from captivity.

Hooks up with other lowlife creatures who smoke cigarettes and tag buildings

Caught in trailer park stealing peanuts. Feigns severe allergic reaction by holding breath until snout turns blue. Escapes as a result.

Meets chipmunks who beat him up and steal all his possessions.

Famished and penniless, he wanders into a traveling circus and lands a job doing high-wire tail tricks.

Stumbles upon the band of chipmunks who robbed him and takes clever revenge.

Buys fancy clothes and meets rich mouse and marries her.

Turns out rich bride is really poor rascal like himself. They part as friends.

Hops boat to next adventure.

Snip of the Tale: A rascal who has a series of loosely connected adventures. His/her peccadilloes seldom lead to serious crime. Because our hero (not) is an unconventional rogue traveling freely and widely, he/she mixes with all classes and is thus capable of social commentary. Novels of this ilk are referred to as picaresque.

SEX IN THE STORY
BY MARY MOUSE ~MM:

Why isn't there sex in our story?

~om:

Most readers like it if it's part of the character's experience and is relevant to the story.

~mm:

I think I just answered that question. Besides, there's only so much you can do with a nursery rhyme—but a limerick, now that's a different story.

~mm:

Snip of the Tale: When handled skillfully, sex can add dimension to the characters and the story—as opposed to a limerick, a poem that is frequently obscene and whose sexual content is for the purpose of bawdy humor.

REVISION

Once there were three mice, a cat, a farmer, and his wife. The mice had no eyesight, yet they decided to chase the tall, skinny woman who was married to the farmer. The woman had a bad temper and suffered from hay fever. She also had a big kitchen knife, and she took aim at their tails as the mice ran by. She cut off their tails.

Three mice who were blind took off after a skinny farmer's wife, who got so mad she grabbed a big, sharp knife and cut off their tails.

Three blind mice ran after the farmer's wife. She cut off their tails with a carving knife.*

*Revision can also lead to longer final drafts.

Quips from the Peanut Gallery

Bogart Mouse:
"Write it again, Sam."

Less is More.
More is Less.
Hold hands, you two,
Clean up this mess.

Chesterton Mouse:
"Murder your darlings."

Pee Wee Mouse:
"Eat lots of pink eraser in the process."

Oscar (Wilde):
"This morning I took out a comma and this afternoon I put it back again."

Draft Dodgers:
See no action, tell no tales.

Snip of the Tale: Most readers never know how many layers of story are behind the one they're reading, but they certainly can feel the roughness of too little sanding and varnish.

TRANSLATION

"Every translation is a betrayal," said Oscar.

"Oh please." Mary slammed her book shut. She thought of all the books she could never have read if it weren't for translators: *The Iliad, Anna K., The Brothers K.*

"Bet you'll like mine," said Pee Wee. Pink eraser was spattered across his snout.

Oscar looked over his shoulder. "A nursery rhyme, that's a cinch."

Mary rolled her red eyes. "It's not so simple. It's a sung text." She belted it out in French just to show the problems of rhythm:

"Trois souris aveugles, regarde comme elles courent!

Elles ont toutes couru après la femme du fermier

Qui leur coupe la queue avec un grand couteau

N'avez-vous jamais vu une telle chose de la vie,

Comme trois souris aveugles?"

"People should learn to speak mouse," said Oscar.

Oh brother. She wondered if there was any point in mentioning the partial solutions posed by computer-assisted translation and translation memory, but just then Pee Wee shouted, "Look! My translation":

Eethray indblay icemay, eesay owhay eythay unray!

Eythay allway anray afterway ethay armerfay'say ifeway,

Owhay utcay offway eirthay ailstay ithway away arvingcay ifeknay,

Idday ouyay everway eesay uchsay away ingthay inway ouryay ifelay,

Asway eethray indblay icemay?

Snip of the Tale: While nothing beats reading a work in its mother tongue, most of us are grateful to faithful translators, who face problems and temptations and yet still find a way to animate a rose by another name and make it nearly as sweet—even in pig Latin. *Olé!*

STYLE

Pee Wee Mouse

Three blind mice ran after the farmer's wife. She cut off their tails with a carving knife.

Dickens Mouse

They were the best of mice, they were the worst of mice, they lived in a cage of despair, they lived in an age of wisdom, they had everything before them in the lab, they had nothing before them in the wild, they were all going to survive, they were all not going to—in short, their lives were so far like the present period of our own. . . .

Homer Mouse

Sing to me of the mice, Muse, the mice of twists and turns driven time and again off course, once they had torched the Love Labs of Inc.

Flannery Mouse

Mary didn't want to go to the country. She wanted to visit some of her connections in East Tennessee and she was seizing at every chance to change Oscar's mind. "Now look here, Oscar," she said, "see here, read this," and she stood with one hand on her thin hip and the other rattling the newspaper at his bald head, right where the electrode had been implanted. "Here this gal that calls herself The Farmer's Wife is aloose from the Federal Pen and you read here what it says she did to these mice. Just you read it."

Hemingway Mouse

Three mice. Woman with knife. No tails.

Dostoyevsky Mouse

We are sick mice. . . . We are spiteful mice. We are unattractive mice. We believe our livers are diseased. However, we know nothing at all about our disease, and do not know for certain what ails us, but we suspect the Spite Coats. That you will probably not understand. Our livers are bad, well—our tails are worse!

Snip of the Tale: It's not just the idea, but the author's way of putting it. Style begins on the level of the sentence, including things like vocabulary, imagery, word order, and length.

PREMISE

NY Lic No. 1dafulPils   DEA# lepOf8th

Herr Doktor Mouse, MD, PhD
Fictional Diagnostician
Central Park Practice
New York, NY 10024
212.555.5555

NAME: _Reader, Generic_

ADDRESS: _Anywhere, USA_ _____ DATE: _02-22-20xx_

Rx

PREMISE   .01 mg

DIRECTIONS: Swallow quickly and follow with a suspension of disbelief.

Contraindications: May not be effective if taken in a state of extreme agitation. Mixing this drug with common over-the-counter formulas may produce a rash of boredom and irritability.

Refill: _prn_

CAUTION: DO NOT OPERATE HEAVY MACHINERY WHILE READING;
READING AT BEDTIME MAY CAUSE DROWSINESS.

Successful clinical trials of Premise include:

> War hero tries for ten years to return home.

> Upper-crust homemaker spends the day planning a party.

> Wealthy shop owner is brought to ruin by her love for a hunchbacked dwarf.

> Novelist becomes obsessed with the beauty of an adolescent boy.

> Man wakes up in the body of a giant bug.

> Hole-dwelling creature with furry toes is sent on an adventure by an old wizard.

> Blind mice chase a farmer's wife.

Snip of the Tale: What the reader needs to accept on faith in order for the story to work.

FLASHBACK

Mary was scampering along the baseboard in the living room when a peculiar smell enveloped her. Suddenly her eyes began to sting and water.

"No!" she yelped, covering her eyes with her paws. She hopped about on her hind legs, panic-stricken.

Oscar grabbed her by the shoulders. "What's the matter?"

"Run for your life!" Mary squealed. "It's the White Coats! They're coming with their chemicals!"

"Calm down. We're not in the lab anymore. It's just one of those stinky plug-in air fresheners."

Snip of the Tale: An event from the past brought back to mind by something in the present. Often deepening our understanding of character, effective flashback has the power to inform the present story line without distracting from it.

COINCIDENCE

"Can you believe our luck?" said Oscar. "The very day we plan our escape, the White Coats forget to lock our cage." Pee Wee and Mary ran to the door. They rattled the bars. Sure enough, the lock fell off.

Snip of the Tale: Events or ideas that occur at the same time and that appear to have a surprising connection but may in fact be random. When a plot depends on too many coincidences, the reader may find the story unbelievable.

FORMULA
THE GREAT HACKWORK BAKE-OFF CONTEST

This year's awards go to Oscar D. Mouse for his WESTERN OMELET; Pee Wee Mouse for his GLAZED DOUGHNUTS; and Mary Mouse for her CHICK'S CHOCOLATE FUDGE recipe.

WESTERN OMELET

Preheat a cast-iron skillet. In a large bowl combine:

> **2–3 bad eggs**
> **1 c. terrorized townsfolk**
> **1 sheriff soaked in alcohol**

Whisk together thoroughly, then add:

> **1 virtuous blonde, of the white-**
> **bread variety to extract the**
> **alcohol**
> **1 tsp. Main Street spices: bank,**
> **saloon, general store, hotel, and**
> **several clove-stick hitching posts**

Pour into skillet and wait for sizzling sound of gunfire to stop. When bad eggs are fried, omelet is finished. Sheriff and blonde have blended happily. Sprinkle with rice.

Remove and serve on tin plate.

Oscar's notes: Variations to this recipe include cattle rustlers who steal from honest ranchers (POACHED EGGS); Indians and US cavalry wage war over territory (BAKED CUSTARD À LA SIOUX CHEF); south-of-the-border outlaw pursued by bounty hunter (HUEVOS RANCHEROS).

GLAZED DOUGHNUTS

Begin with a large quantity of water and wait for yeasty body to rise to the surface. Combine:

> **1 cop-turned-detective**
> **1 c. all-purpose captain or DA to impose restrictions**
> **Zest of cunning killer**

Mix well, then blend in:

> **6 tbs. buttery clues**
> **¼ c. sugary distractions**
> **3 eggs**

Stir vigorously. If clues do not pan out, drink and smoke cigarettes while waiting for more bodies to rise. When dough has doubled in size, transfer mixture to flat, floury surface. Slap around a bit, then roll out to ½ inch thick. Examine the texture of the dough. You will notice that the killer has left a firm clue. Finally, seeing what you kneaded, the DA agrees to give you a well-floured doughnut cutter. With it, punch several holes into center of killer's identity and whereabouts.

Fry 2–3 clues quickly in bubbling fat at 360°F.

Drain on paper towel. Catch the full scent and begin a hot pursuit. Get burned for effect but not destroyed. Fry killer in the process. Back at the station, make topping. Mix:

> **1 c. powdered sugar**
> **3 tbs. water**

Glaze the warm doughnuts and savor sweetness while waiting for next case.

Pee Wee's Notes: For variety, try buddy cops solve crime (follow FRENCH TWIST recipe—sprinkle with an extra blonde or brunette so no one thinks they're gay); retiring cop's one unsolved case (follow JELLY ROLL recipe); small-town crooked sheriff (follow BEIGNET recipe then slather with slang). Nothing beats glazed doughnuts topped with silver sprinkles. Shiny, shiny, all miney.

CHICK'S CHOCOLATE FUDGE

Combine in a heavy-bottomed saucepan:

Girl made of 2 c. sugar

Boy made of ¼ c. corn syrup and ⅛ tsp. salt

½ c. heavy cream to follow

Stir over low heat about 5 minutes, then add:

1 tsp. vanilla bliss

Separate girl and boy. Cry a little and add salt from tears. Brush down the sides of the pan and remove from heat. Stir until melted and completely smooth:

6 oz. bittersweet chocolate

Return to heat and cook until it reaches 238°F, the soft-ball stage, then remove from burner. Add but do not stir in (stirring at this point can cause graininess):

2 tbs. of soft, sweet butter

When it is cool, stir the fudge with a wooden spoon just until it "snaps" and begins to lose its sheen, then reunite boy and girl. How sweet it tastes.

Mary's Notes: The girl/boy recipe (now available in same-sex dramas) includes various degrees of winning and losing each other: (a) often through their own folly, e.g., mistaken belief the other is not interested (see CHOCOLATE TRIFLE recipe); or (b) through the intervention of others, e.g., a bitter rival (see CHOCOLATE CHIP COOKIE) or family members (see CAPULET CHOCOLATE TORTE). In my opinion, nothing beats a good love story, although I would not admit this publicly.

TTT CONTEST DISCLAIMER:

We recognize that "formula" is a pejorative term for baking that lacks originality. On the other hand, formulas are a staple of cooking. A good chef brings her own style, energy, imagination, hard work, and 1 percent luck to the same old food, the way George Crum did in 1853 when he turned the lowly potato into potato chips.

Snip of the Tale: For better or for worse, we follow and depend on formulas all our lives. The reader counts on the staple ingredients of a good love story, thriller, or Western for a satisfying reading experience in that genre. Once in a while someone bangs two stones together and a whole new genre ignites, as in Truman Capote's *In Cold Blood*.

CLICHÉ

When the cat's away, the mouse will play.

Are you a man or a mouse?

Quiet as a mouse.

Build a better mousetrap and the world will beat a path to your door.

Hotter than a mouse in a wool sock.

Poor as a church mouse.

Is that a mouse in your pocket, or are you just happy to see me?

Busier than a one-eyed cat watching two mouse holes.

Snip of the Tale: A once lively phrase now worn out from use.

SENTENCE DIAGRAM
MARY'S PRESENT TO AUNT GERTY

Three blind mice ran after the farmer's wife.

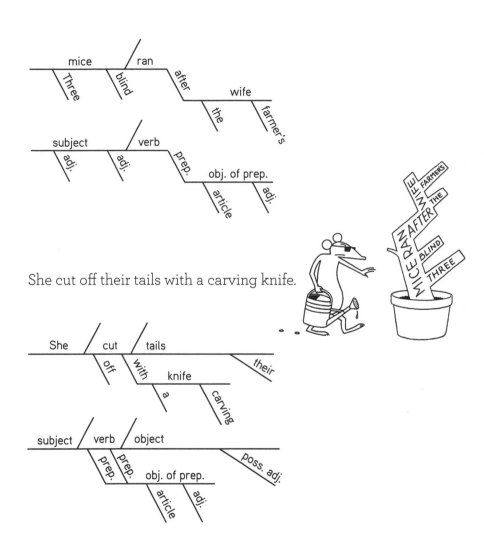

She cut off their tails with a carving knife.

Snip of the Tale: Depending on your optic, diagramming sentences is an old form of torture or a delightful way to play with language.

HERO (NOT)

"Mary, you're my heroine."

Oscar's cheek twitched, pulling back the corner of one side of his mouth. "Addicted to your sister, eh?"

"Cheap," said Mary, "even for you."

Pee Wee scratched his fur. "What does that mean?"

"Nothing," said Mary. She squinted and gave Oscar a beady stare. Her whiskers quivered. "Oscar's just being smart. You see, many people don't use the term 'hero' or 'heroine' anymore."

"So what should I say?"

"Protagonist." Oscar picked at his teeth with a piece of matchstick, then examined the goodies. "Anyway, she's more along the lines of what one would call an antihero. She's not as virtuous as she seems."

"Are you kidding? She's greater than Mighty Mouse."

"Thank you, Pee Wee." Mary reached across the table and patted Pee Wee's paw. "But—"

"*Puh*-lease, no one even knows who Mighty Mouse is anymore, and do you know why? You can only beat up so many cats and save so many helpless mice before you seem like some god on Mount Gouda who's not really connected to the average *Mus musculus* and vice versa."

"I never said I was perfect," said Mary.

"You try to act like you are. Do-gooder. Thoughtful. Confident. Sometimes you are. Sometimes you aren't."

"Not true," said Pee Wee. "She always knows the right thing to do. And she *is* a do-gooder. Remember when our tails got cut off? Right away she got the bread-wrapper wires and made tourniquets. We would have bled to death without Mary's quick thinking."

"Oscar's right," said Mary. "I'm not always as good as I would like people to think. I have my faults."

"You and the San Andreas."

Mary ignored that. She knew that even Superman occasionally got kryptonite in his shorts. His shier self was a bit myopic and not so suave with the ladies as his blue-tighted double.

$\mathcal{S}$nip of the Tale: Today's hero is likely to have as many, if not more, foibles than we as readers see in ourselves, and as a result such characters seldom lord it over us like they used to.

DESCRIPTION
JUST THE (SIGNIFICANT) FACTS, MA'AM

Mouse	Mary	Oscar	Pee Wee
Length	3.2" plus 2.8" tail	3.4" plus 3.8" tail	2.9" plus 2.4" tail
Weight	25 g	36 g	20 g
Eye color	Red	Brown	Reddish brown
Vibrisse	Fine whiskers	Submental and interramal hairs that resemble a Fu Manchu	I wish—although I've got a couple genal strands and my superciliary lashes are quite long
Scars	Punch holes in ears	Keloid on cranium	Burn marks on the walking pads of both fore and hind paws
Other distinguishing features	10 mammae :::::	Protruding incisors ||	Face often freckled with particles of pink eraser

"Hey." Oscar looked over Pee Wee's shoulder. "It's supposed to be description, not a police report. And why are you telling everyone about my scar"—Oscar didn't like anyone knowing he had an electrode planted in his brain—"and my prominent incisors?"

"Buckteeth," said Pee Wee. Oscar slapped him in the back of the head.

Mary dropped the sunflower seed she was nibbling. "'Protruding incisors' should stay. You couldn't have chewed those insulated wires that led to our escape without them."

"Sure thing, Ten Mammae."

"Mammae?" Mary darted over to look. She slapped the back of Pee Wee's head too. "My mammae have nothing to do with the story. It's not like I've had a litter in the last fourteen weeks."

"If my buckteeth stay," said Oscar, "so do your mammae."

Snip of the Tale: A picturing verbally. Like dialogue and action, good description often moves the story forward.

REPETITION REPETITION REPETITION REPETITION REPETITION
REPETITION REPETITION REPETITION REPETITION REPETITION

Mary, Oscar, and Pee Wee went out in a boat.
Oscar fell over.
Who was left?

Mary and Pee Wee went out in a boat.
Mary fell over.
Who was left?

Pee Wee gawped at the boat.
No way. He sent
His shadow.

Pee Wee's shadow tripled in size.
Now ponder its demise—
Sunset or capsize?

Snip of the Tale: The pleasure of repetition
from the acoustic to the unconscious is
ubiquitous. It has great power in almost any art
form, yet too much repetition seems tedious.

PROLOGUE
PROLOGUE TO *THRICE TOLD TALES*

Before Oscar, Mary, and Pee Wee were captured and sold to Love Your Face Laboratory, Inc., they had many adventures. Not all of them were pleasant, but let's not talk about those. Mary spent most of her time in the library reading and gnawing on books. She now has a tremendous range of knowledge, which she puts to good use in the pages that follow. Oscar spent much of his time as a vagabond working peculiar jobs. Although you'd never catch him in a library, he does read. His favorite thing next to the Bard is Spider-Man comics. He's not very nice to his sister or brother, although if you twisted his paw, he would admit that he does love them. The youngest is Pee Wee, and he's fond of nibbling on pink erasers, especially when he writes. Secretly he wants to be a writer. He hoards shiny things like a dragon; this sometimes gets him into trouble. All three of them detest the White Coats.

CHAPTER 1

Snip of the Tale: A term often associated with drama. Written by the author. In books the prologue is part of the front matter, which precedes chapter 1. It contains information specifically related to the story in some way; may contain backstory.

UNRELIABLE NARRATORS
FAVORITE SNACK FOODS

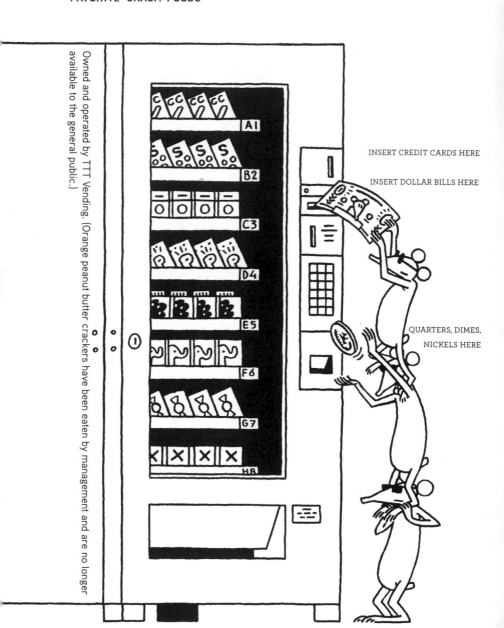

INSERT CREDIT CARDS HERE

INSERT DOLLAR BILLS HERE

QUARTERS, DIMES,
NICKELS HERE

Owned and operated by TTT Vending. (Orange peanut butter crackers have been eaten by management and are no longer available to the general public.)

A1 *Child's Candy*

B2 *Skittles for the Insane*

C3 *Breath Mints for the Intoxicated*

D4 *Pop Rocks for Quarreling Lovers*

E5 *Doper's Brownies*

F6 *Elephant Crackers for the Six Men of Indostan*

G7 *Liar's Taffy*

H8 *Nothing for the Severely Depressed*

Snip of the Tale: A narrator not to be completely trusted due to his or her limitations. (A five-year-old's reasoning is not the same as yours, oh mature reader.)

SIMILE, METAPHOR, AND CONCEIT

Simile
Pee Wee turned as white as snow when Oscar shut him in the freezer.

Metaphor
Matilda's arm was a bolt of lightning; the mice didn't stand a chance.

Conceit
Mice are like weeds: They grow just about anywhere, people do their best to get rid of them, but when looked at closely, they can be truly appealing.

Snip of the Tale: All three are forms of comparison. A comparison using "like" or "as" is called a simile. A direct comparison (without "like" or "as") is called a metaphor. A conceit is an extended comparison of two very unlikely things (and can make use of direct and indirect forms of comparison).

FRAME STORY
THE MATRYOSHKA NESTING DOLL

Oscar cited these "framous" examples:

> *The Arabian Nights,*
> *The Canterbury Tales,*
> *The Decameron,* and
> *The Book of the City of Ladies*

All these have stories within stories.

Mary held up her paw and wiggled each digit, citing more-contemporary examples:

> *Heart of Darkness,*
> *The Great Gatsby,*
> *Frankenstein,* and
> *The Turn of the Screw—*

which, by the end, becomes an unhinged frame, but still.
   All these have stories within stories.

Now it was Pee Wee's turn. He held up a matryoshka doll. The outside figure was of his adult self. But when he began to disassemble the doll, nesting inside each one was a younger version of himself. The last one, a pinkie with no hair, didn't open.
   Within the adult self are many stories of the younger self.

Snip of the Tale: A story within a story.

DETAIL

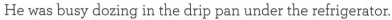

Pee Wee nudged Oscar. "Did you hear that?"

Oscar ignored him.

He was busy dozing in the drip pan under the refrigerator.

Pee Wee shook him harder.

Oscar yawned and twitched his whiskers. "Hear what?"

"That scuffing noise. There it is again." Pee Wee flattened himself against the floor and scuttled toward the front of the refrigerator. Large red and gray checked cylinders were headed straight for them. Protruding from one of them was the head of a scaly serpent, vaguely brown with bluish bumps and hairs and a yellowish shield covering what must surely be its face. "Oscar, come quick! The thing I told you about before is back."

The cylinders stopped right at the edge of the refrigerator. The serpent rose up and wiggled its body, sniffing the air.

Pee Wee closed his eyes and whispered over and over again, "I hope it can't smell us. I hope it can't smell us. I hopeitcan'tsmellus."

Right then the refrigerator door opened and illuminated the beast.

"You wantwit," said Oscar. He slapped Pee Wee in the back of the head. "Those are her slippers. And that's her toe, not a serpent. And that's her toenail, not a shield." Oscar crawled back to the drip pan. He had to admit that the toe did indeed look like a creature from another universe, but having already slapped Pee Wee, he thought it best not to lose face by agreeing with him now.

Snip of the Tale: Details are necessary to develop character, setting, and situation, but they must also be details that *matter*. Begin by appealing to the senses.

DIALECT, AIN'T IT?

Oscar's wanderlust led him deep into the hills of mouse country, where he recorded the following conversation in his journal:

> Ain't got no Gouda, is ya?
>> Ain't said I ain't.
>> Ain't asked ya ain't ya ain't, asked ya
>> ain't ya is, is ya?

Snip of the Tale: Form of a spoken language that is particular to a region, or a social or occupational group.

EPISTOLARY NOVEL

Dear Evelina,

I am so fortunate to have a friend like you in whom I can confide. It's been hard for all of us to lose our tails, especially Pee Wee. Since we left the farmhouse, we've been living in various locations, none of them ideal. Oscar keeps arguing for us to return to the farmhouse, where life was grand before the tragedy. He says we're smarter now with hindsight and won't get hurt again. What should we do?

Best friends forever,
~mm:

Dear Mary,

Did the farmer's wife cut off part of Oscar's brain, too? Who in their right mind would return to such a place? You will find another fine dwelling before too long, full of crumbs and dark nesting places. I hope Pee Wee is feeling better. And Mary, you really haven't told me anything about yourself. Are you dating anyone? They're not all rats, you know.

BFF,
xEvelina

Dear Evelina,

I'm still worried about Pee Wee. He seems so fragile and has stopped talking to me. Does he feel he can no longer confide in his own sister? Although we try to keep Pee Wee out of our arguments, Oscar and I are still fighting about whether or not to move back to the farmhouse; we may move back, as I'm so worn down arguing about it. And since you asked, my love life, sadly, is pretty nonexistent; it's hard to have confidence when one is missing one's tail.

As always,
~mm:

Dear Mary,

Are you crazy? Do not move back to that farmhouse! I mean it! About Pee Wee: Sometimes it is easier to talk to someone other than a family member. Maybe I should write to him. The most important thing is that he has someone to talk to. Tail or no tail, you are a sweet mouse, and any Mus worth its whiskers would be fortunate to have someone like you. You are also sophisticated, another reason not to move back to the country, where they hunt with knives—how uncivilized!

WBS,
xxEvelina

Snip of the Tale: A novel written in the form of letters by the character(s). Today, more broadly, it might be thought to include e-mail and other contemporary forms of correspondence.

DICTION

Three blind mice ran after the farmer's wife. She cut off their tails with a carving knife.

A trio of myopic pests pursued the spouse of the agriculturalist. She severed their appendages with a blade.

Mary, Pee Wee, and Oscar ran after Matilda Bethoon. She cut off their tails.

Yo. Check it out. Them Stuart Littles messed with that lady one too many times. She unhinged their caboose. Ain't nothing bringing up the rear. That's cold.

Three members of the Muridae family scurried toward a *Homo sapiens* of the female variety. She excised their caudae.

Three mice. I say, three mice. I say, three mice ran after the farmer's wife. The wife. I say, the wife. I say, the farmer's wife cut off their tails. She did it with a knife.

Snip of the Tale: Word choice.

SYMBOLISM
WHITE COATS

Pee Wee stood up on his hind legs, his paws batting at the wire partition. "They're coming! Run!"

"Run? Where? Between the wires of the cage?" With that, Oscar pulled Pee Wee into the corner farthest from the door. Shivering, they held each other as a White Coat bent down and fumbled with the latch.

In the other corner Mary quivered beneath shredded paper. Her eyes were still red and swollen from the White Coat's previous visit. "Which one this time? Skinny four-eyes?"

"What difference does it make?" Oscar rubbed the raised scar on his head, where an electrode had been implanted. "They're all sadists."

Snip of the Tale: A symbol is itself (white coat) and a stand-in for something else (cruelty). In another context a white coat could represent healing or perhaps knowledge.

POINT OF VIEW

First Person

Raisin, yummy! That's the last thing I remember thinking as I climbed out of the toaster and ran toward Mary and Oscar, when swiftly, out of nowhere—*chop. Chop, chop.*

Second Person

You wake up, and to your surprise you crawl out of bed on all fours.

Hovering over you is an enormous mouse with buckteeth who says, "You look like you just saw a cat." You squeak. Somehow he understands and says: "Come on." For reasons you can't explain you run out in time to see an ugly giant wielding an enormous knife.

Third Person (Omniscient)

Mary couldn't shake the feeling that something bad was about to happen at the farmhouse, but Pee Wee and Oscar were having the time of their lives. Oscar bathed in the drip pan of the refrigerator while counting all the cheeses he had tasted. Meanwhile, Pee Wee found a raisin, and it took all of his willpower to save half of it to show Mary and Oscar. He was running when Matilda saw him and reached for her knife. She had had enough! "Take that. And that. And that."

Third Person (Limited Omniscient)

Oscar was soaking in the drip pan. The water felt relaxing, and he counted all the cheeses he had ever tasted. When he got to the *v*'s, he thought about the farmer's wife, who bought only Velveeta. Feeling hungry, he slipped out from under the refrigerator to see Pee Wee racing by, a look of terror on his face. But it was too late. *Chop. Chop. Chop.*

Third Person (Objective/Reportorial)

A mouse came crawling out of the toaster with something round and dark between its teeth. A woman was chopping vegetables at the opposite counter. She turned with a knife in her hand and looked at the mouse. The mouse jumped off the counter and ran. Two other mice came out from underneath the refrigerator. The woman wielded her knife. *Chop. Chop. Chop.*

Snip of the Tale: How the author presents the story. Above, Pee Wee tells his own story in first person; second person demands that you, the reader, become the character; then three examples of third person: (a) omniscient (all-knowing), (b) limited omniscient (less than all-knowing—usually in the mind of one or two characters), and lastly, (c) objective or reportorial (only those things that can be objectively observed). In sum, the "vantage point" the writer uses to tell the story.

BEGINNING

MULTIPLE-CHOICE QUIZ

Nom de plume: _____

Directions: You know the drill.

1. For the reader, the beginning of a story is
   a. page 1 (if there's no prologue)
   b. same as above

2. For the writer, the beginning of a story is
   a. "Three blind mice"
   b. the prologue
   c. page 1
   d. something that comes after several rewrites
   e. actually the ending (work backward)
   f. #!*&%# ahhhhhr rats!
   g. not something you should really think about while doing
   h. could be one or more of the above, plus gobs more

h.

~~mm:

No talking during a test.

:O~~

Snip of the Tale: For the reader, the beginning starts on page 1; for the writer, the beginning may start somewhere else.

SUSPENSE

Three blind mice run after the farmer's wife. She screams and runs. They chase her around the table and back toward the kitchen counter, where she picks up a knife.

Yikes! Now she chases them. They squeal and run past her into the living room. She swings the knife—just as the mice run under a footrest—and cuts the leather on the stool. While she's trying to dislodge the knife, the mice run back into the kitchen and into the broom closet. Now she has them cornered and swings again.

They dart between her legs. The feel of their fur makes her cringe with horror and drop the knife.

Oscar bites her right ankle. Mary and Pee Wee sink their teeth into the left one. She tumbles. She's bleeding but manages to get up. The chase resumes.

Around and around the table they go. The pursuit leads back to the kitchen counter, where she grabs another knife. . . .

Snip of the Tale: What will happen next? In particular, what will happen to a character we care about? Conversely, what will happen to one we don't care about but hope will get his/her comeuppance?

STEREOTYPE

Mice love cheese.
Mice carry disease.

Snip of the Tale: A presentation of character that is too simple and thus invites the reader to judge her/him based on that simplification.

EXPOSITION
TWO EXAMPLES

Oscar stood with the two wires in his hand. It was almost as thrilling as the first time he felt the wooden stick of a match, its red tip gliding along the friction strip—the sudden flare of blue, then red fire. And the smell . . . His fascination with fire had led him to learn all about combustion methods. He looked at the petri dish below. Once he crossed the wires and dropped them, the accelerant inside would take over and they'd all be free.

or:

Mary's passion for reading dated back to her early mousehood, when her mother moved into a public library that had closed for lack of funding. There, undisturbed, she had worked her way up through picture books to young adult fiction and finally to just about anything she could get her paws on and teeth into. Her dedication to learning proved to be invaluable when she was captured and imprisoned in a laboratory cage. She was able to entertain herself and her siblings by devouring every word fit to print in the newspapers that lined their cage, until her vision went.

Snip of the Tale: Information we need to know in order to understand the present story line. This is akin to backstory, and it works best when the writer strategically places the information throughout the story.

RESEARCH
WHENCE COMETH THAT RHYME?

Wait, Dear Reader, do I look like a jump rope? No skipping over me! Here's one of the best parts (and something not that many people know) about the history of this rhyme. So keep reading and we'll end with the beginning, which is, well, way cool.

Here is the round that many of us are familiar with as it appears in *The Oxford Dictionary of Nursery Rhymes* (1952, 1997), edited by Iona and Peter Opie:

> *Three blind mice, see how they run!*
> *They all ran after the farmer's wife,*
> *Who cut off their tails with a carving knife,*
> *Did you ever see such a thing in your life,*
> *As three blind mice?*

[In *The Annotated Mother Goose: Nursery Rhymes Old and New* (1962) the round differs from the above in the fourth line only, which reads: "Did you ever see such a sight in your life."]

The earliest recorded version appeared in 1609 in *Deuteromelia; or, The Second part of Musicks melodie.* The editor and, according to scholars Peter and Iona Opie, probable part author was Thomas Ravenscroft, still a teenager at the time.

> *Three blinde Mice, three blinde Mice,*
> *Dame Iulian, Dame Iulian,*
> *the Miller and his merry olde Wife,*
> *shee scrapte her tripe licke thou the knife.*

There has been some suggestion that the rhyme is of political origin and that the farmer's wife is a stand-in for Queen Mary

I (a staunch Catholic known as Bloody Mary) and the mice, for Protestant noblemen burned at the stake for conspiring against the queen. While undisputed evidence exists that links nursery rhymes to political and historical events in England, I found no solid evidence to support such a connection in the case of the three blind mice.

The rhyme made its first appearance on the nursery scene of children's literature in 1842 with the publication of James Orchard Halliwell's *The Nursery Rhymes of England.* He knew only three lines of the rhyme at the time, and it wasn't until the following year that the fourth line, "Did you ever see such fools in your life," was added. A concluding footnote on the topic in *The Oxford Dictionary of Nursery Rhymes* cites quite a different version, one (in *Notes and Queries*, 1890) that goes back three generations:

> *Three blind mice,*
> *See how they run,*
> *A farmer married an ugly wife,*
> *And she cut her throat with a carving knife,*
> *Did you ever see such a fool in your life,*
> *Three blind mice.*

An equally interesting version prior to 1860, in which no violence occurs, is cited by Gloria T. Delamar in *Mother Goose, from Nursery to Literature* (1987):

Three blind mice, three blind mice,
Ran around thrice, ran around thrice,
The miller and his merry old wife,
N'er laughed so much in all their life.

In *The Christian Mother Goose Book of Nursery Rhymes* (2001), Marjorie Ainsborough Decker has, for the most part, converted the Mother Goose characters to Christianity. The three blind mice are "three kind mice," who are helpful to all in word and deed. (Fear not, Dear Reader, even for Humpty Dumpty, who shouts, "Amen! / God can put me together again.")

For the more deliciously discerning appetite, there's no beating *The Eventful History of Three Blind Mice* (a book adapted from the 1858 version, *The Eventful History of Three Little Mice and How They Became Blind*). Although the author is unknown, the illustrator with whom she/he conspires is a young Winslow Homer. It is a book, writes Maurice Sendak in the introduction, that "literally gets away with murder," and the "extraordinary images" foreshadow the picture book form we know today. Drawn to the book by his interest in Homer, Sendak confesses to falling in love with the story and suspects Homer fell a little in love with it too.

I hope, Dear Reader, that you have fallen a little in love as well.

Snip of the Tale: As readers, we take pleasure in learning new things and we hope that writers—particularly of fiction—do their homework. Background research into a text to enrich a re-creation, or accuracy of specific details, all matter. If we know that ether made its way into surgery in the mid-1840s, we lose faith in a writer's story when a doctor in Caesar's army is administering it to operate on the wounded.

DEUS EX MACHINA

The stubs of their tails were healing nicely; their spirits were another story entirely.

"I'm not me anymore," moaned Pee Wee.

Oscar slipped off the edge of the empty sardine can on which he'd been perched. "My balance is shot. I almost wish a snap trap had gotten me instead of the knife."

Just then Mary scampered under the refrigerator toward them, dragging a fragment of newspaper. She dropped it in front of them and ran over it several times, flattening it with her paws. "Read this!"

All three leaned over the scrap of newspaper.

Miracle Berry Discovered in the Amazon

An exotic jungle berry known as **Deus ex machina** has been shown to have extraordinary regenerative powers. Several mice, having lost various body parts through accidents or experimentation, have regrown what they had thought lost forever after drinking the juice of this berry.

Act now and for a limited time only you will receive two bottles for the price of one, an offer almost unheard of. Remember that **Deus ex machina** is the only product endorsed by the hand of God himself. No other formula can make this claim. Act now. Your mice are depending on your contrived intervention.

Snip of the Tale: A sudden, unlikely resolution to a problem or conflict that seems to come from nowhere, if not "descending from the gods," as was often the case in ancient Greek drama.

CHARACTER
ROUND AND FLAT

Mary, Pee Wee, and Oscar were sitting around the candle flame, gnawing on coffee beans. Mary had eaten two already and had the shakes. She and Oscar had been up for hours trying to help Pee Wee grapple with the subject of character.

Mary had come up with this:

o —

Oscar had come up with this:

∿∿O:

Snip of the Tale: While all characters are generally based on the moral makeup of human personality and behavior, some appear as flat, without human complexity, and others emerge fully formed and ready to trot. We don't want the UPS driver who delivers the package to the main character taking center stage—but wait, maybe for a sec he does, and then he flattens again.

PATHETIC FALLACY

Pee Wee studied his writers' correspondence-course manual for the definition of "pathetic fallacy." Happily, the book had suggested a mnemonic device to help him remember (sung to the tune of "Frère Jacques").

Frère Jacques	*Pathetic Fallacy*
Frère Jacques,	**The name given**
Frère Jacques,	**The name given**
Dormez vous?	**to your met-**
Dormez vous?	**to your met-**
Sonnez les matines!	**metaphors**
Sonnez les matines!	**when they suck.**
Din, dan, don.	**Din, dan, don**
Din, dan, don.	**Din, dan, don.**

Three of Jacques's sucking metaphors:

From the department of cliché: "Ruby lips."

From the department of lacking any sensibility: "The victim's postmortem lividity was the same color as blueberry cupcakes."

From the augmentation department: "His ankle swelled up until it looked like a mottled pomegranate, an apple, a bruised persimmon."

Snip of the Tale: "Pathetic fallacy" is a term coined by John Ruskin to describe the giving of human emotions to nature. It is also the name sometimes given to metaphors when they fail.

BILDUNGSROMAN

Mary stood up on her hind legs and stretched. The matchbox that served as her desk was covered with bits of paper, on which Pee Wee had been scratching out the revisions of his novel, *It's Such a Hard Life*.

"You know," she yawned, "what you're writing is really a bildungsroman."

Pee Wee spit out a storm of pink eraser flakes. "A what?"

"A bildungsroman."

"Haven't you been paying any attention? I'm writing about *me*, not buildings."

Mary squeaked a laugh. "You're writing about the adventures of a young *Mus musculus* as he becomes an adult. That makes it a bildungsroman, *Roman* meaning a 'novel,' and *Bildung* meaning 'development.' It's a German word."

"I'm writing in *Mus*glish," said Pee Wee, "not German."

"Oh brother."

Snip of the Tale: A bildungsroman can be thought of as a coming-of-age story—often the main character is an adolescent on the verge of adulthood.

DENOUEMENT
THE GREAT MOUSE DETECTIVE EXPLAINS

"Okay, Great Mouse Detective, it's already been explained to me how—if the mice were really blind—they could see to chase the farmer's wife. And I get *why* she cut off their tails—because she was a sadist. But explain to me *how* someone as tall as the farmer's wife could lean over so quickly and simultaneously cut off all three tails."

"Elementary, my slender ort of a reader: She dove!"

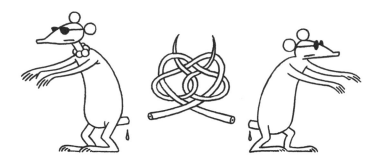

$\int$nip of the Tale: "Denouement" is literally "an unknotting" and refers to that part of the story where the plot complications are undone and the reader finally finds out what's what. The crisis has already occurred and the story is moving toward a resolution.

FABLE

When Pee Wee Mouse dropped a raisin, he knew he was doomed. Cat opened one sleepy eye and thrust her paw down on Pee Wee's tail. "Well, well," said Cat, "I wake up and lunch is served."

"Please don't eat me," said Pee Wee. "I could be of use to you someday."

At that Cat laughed so hard that her pointed teeth shone. "You amuse me," said Cat. "I just might let you live." In truth, Cat had just eaten a bird not an hour before and was not hungry, or she would have eaten Pee Wee straightaway whether he amused her or not. In an instant she retracted her claws and swatted him across the floor with her paw. "Get."

Pee Wee didn't have to be told twice. He ran.

About a week later Pee Wee heard a horrible mewing and saw that Cat was in great distress. She had been swatting at a bumblebee, and it had stung her in the middle of her back, leaving a big stinger. She scratched, but scratching only made it worse.

"I'll help you," said Pee Wee, "if you let me." He climbed up her back and dug around in her fur until he found the sharp, long stinger and plucked it out.

Cat felt relief immediately and a quiver ran through her body. "Well," she said, "little friends may prove mighty friends after all."

Snip of the Tale: A tale that often uses animals as characters, whose conversation and actions make a point of teaching us something. The tale above plays off Aesop's fables.

PARABLE
PEE WEE AND THE GIRL (RIFFING OFF RUMI)

Pee Wee once caught hold of the shoelaces of a little girl as she walked about the meadow.

"Woo-hoo!" he shouted. "Check it out, everybody." He thought because he had hold of her shoestrings, he was pulling her along. "I am one strong *Mus*." As if to prove it, he held on to the rope with one paw. With his other paw he blew on his nails and buffed them against his furry chest.

Naturally, the girl was walking by herself, which seemed obvious, though not to Pee Wee.

Presently they arrived at a fast-moving stream, and Pee Wee stopped. He stopped pulling the laces. He stopped chewing the aglets. He stopped his gleeful blustering.

The girl looked down at her shoes. "Why have you stopped, little mouse? I thought you were my guide. Please continue."

"B-b-but," said Pee Wee, "I might drown in this torrent."

"Hmm," said the little girl. She stuck her other foot into the stream and water rose up to the middle of her calf. "It's not so high. Go on."

"I-i-it's nothing to you," squeaked Pee Wee, "but I'll surely drown."

The girl took pity on Pee Wee, who after all was very sweet and cute. And, she noticed, very scared. "Climb up on my shoulder, then. And next time, don't—"

"Believe me," said Pee Wee. "I won't."

Snip of the Tale: A parable generally uses people in a realistic setting. As with fable, there's a message or lesson to be taught, though what the message is tends to be cryptic and open to interpretation.

MYTH
HOW THE MOUSE CAME TO HAVE A LONG TAIL

When the world was very new and the sun shiny as a copper penny, man came out of the caves and forced the beasts of burden to work for him. The oxen plowed the fields. The donkeys brought in the harvest crops on their backs, but the mice did nothing except wait in the storage shed for corn and grain.

One night Cat crept into the light of the campfire and said, "If you let me take shelter in your granary, in return I will take care of your problem."

Man said, "Even if I agreed to let you stay, they're too fast, you'll never catch them."

The first moon came and went; Cat caught nothing. He'd lie in wait and then pounce. His claws came back empty. But Cat was patient. Eventually he caught the mice with ease, and his belly was so full that his contentment led to boredom. One evening he slapped down his paw on the rear of Mouse and watched with amusement as Mouse tried to escape. Cat would lift his paw and almost let Mouse escape, then slap it down again, kneading poor Mouse like dough. In the end Mouse's skin began to stretch and grow, until a long, thin tail formed that was so narrow at the end Mouse finally slipped through Cat's claws.

And that is how the mouse came to have such a long tail.

Snip of the Tale: Myths attempt to explain events in nature—how the world was created and by whom, how humans and other life forms came to be as they are. Gods and heroes are common. Like existentialism, myths often search for explanations about why we exist, our meaning and place in the world, and mortality and death.

MISE-EN-SCÈNE
THE KITCHEN

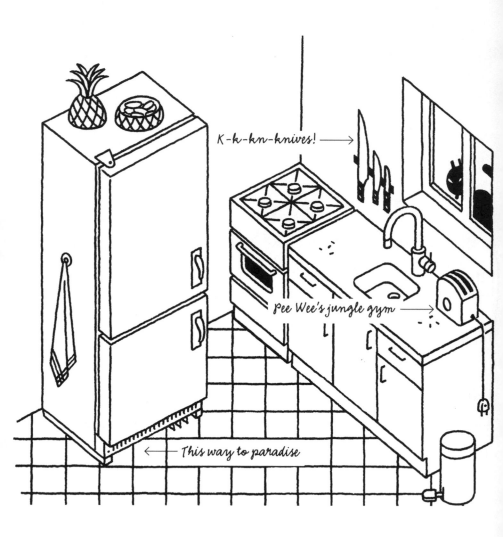

K-k-kn-knives! →

Pee Wee's jungle gym →

← This way to paradise

Snip of the Tale: Broadly, this refers to how something is arranged on stage. Viewers can see it clearly. When you read, however, the onus is on the writer to make an important scene just as vivid as in a play.

ROMAN À CLEF
EXCERPTED FROM *ME AND MACKEY*, BY OSCAR D. MOUSE

From the time we were pinkies it was clear to Ma that Mackey Mouse was special. How, I'll never know. He was a gangly-looking little thing with spaghetti legs and the roundest ears you ever did see. Even back then he had a high, squeaky voice and laughed like he'd swallowed a mouthful of helium. I knew him before he ever came to fame and ended up living in that magical castle.

In those early days he was poor like me, and we cut our incisors on aglets because no one could afford melba toast. I'm talking the dirt-poor twenties, when we all slept on beds of chewed newspaper.

Mackey never had a Ma of his own, and his Daddy spent most of his time drawing at a desk. Mackey had nothing to do but scratch his lice (of which he had plenty). One afternoon I befriended him and took him home to hang around our hole in the wall. We didn't have much food, but Ma always said, "What's one more sunflower seed?" He fit right in immediately, and when Pa and the others played the harmonica and blew into the Tabasco bottle, Mackey got to dancing and whistling and shaking his hips, to the delight of all in the room, and if you've ever seen him in his debut performance of *Steamboat Billy*, you know just what I'm talking about. Ma said, "That varmint is gonna go places. . . ."

Snip of the Tale: A thinly disguised novel based on the lives of well-known figures.

AMBIGUITY

Mary

Mary got to the last chapter of *Mt. Everest Adventures*. It had been one disaster after another. Dehydration. Supplies lost. Bickering over who would be the first to the summit. Then, "the accident." Mary closed the book and said: "I'm not confused, I'm just not sure if he meant to let go of the rope his buddy depended on, or if he just couldn't hold on anymore."

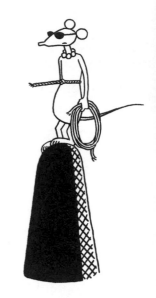

Oscar

Oscar perused a psychology book, looking for optical illusions. He stopped when he came to a stark black-and-white picture. Was it a vase or two faces?

Pee Wee

In his mind Pee Wee was jumping double Dutch with words. Whoopee, everybody. Welcome to my brain. Double Dutch. Double word Dutch. Does *clip* fasten or cut? Does *buckle* break or bind? Does *adumbrate* clarify or cast a shadow? Does *scan* mean a close look or a glance? Does *overlook* mean to watch over or fail to notice? If you *weather*, do you withstand or wear away?

Snip of the Tale: When ambiguity (open to more than one interpretation) is intentional, we as readers are left to think about the possible outcomes or meanings long after we set the book aside.

VERISIMILITUDE

"That word is almost as big a word as 'bildungsroman,'" said Pee Wee.

Mary thought for a moment. "It just means 'the appearance of truth.'"

"In magic," said Oscar, "that would be called illusion. You make something seem real."

"Let's say you decide to make a map," Mary said.

"A treasure map." Pee Wee thumped his paws together. "Oh goodie."

"Any map. Say you make a map of this house. Only for the sake of truth and accuracy you decide to make the map as big as the house itself and include every single piece of furniture. It may be accurate, but it wouldn't be helpful."

"I'll say." Oscar twirled a whisker. "Imagine folding and unfolding it. You'd need a hundred mice to help."

"But compress and reduce the scale, include a couple of key pieces of furniture, and it seems to reflect the truth. The user can quickly find her way to your treasure."

"My treasure. No one better touch my stash." Pee Wee suddenly wanted to race to his pile of goodies to be sure his cache was still there.

Snip of the Tale: The reader doesn't need every detail or moment accounted for. By giving us the key details of character, setting, and compressed moments of time, an impression of truth is created that seems real to us.

CATHARSIS
IN WHICH THEIR OWN TALE IS TOO CLOSE TO HOME TO PURGE

Pee Wee pounced on the remote and tuned in the movie *Chicken Run*. In the course of the movie, he bit his nail, cried, and got angry and afraid. Near the end, when the chickens escape the coop and the hatchet fate that awaits them—and in an airplane, no less—Pee Wee cheered. Credits rolled. "I feel exhilarated."

Oscar spit a popcorn kernel across the room. "The farmer's ending did it for me. Ax to you, Green Jeans."

"It's terrible to say that," added Mary, "but I felt good too. Almost like taking a shower at the end of a long day."

Snip of the Tale: An emotional cleansing that is sometimes experienced by a viewer or reader of a movie, opera, play, or book, etc.

ALLUSION

After the three blind mice had lost their tails to the farmer's wife, Oscar said: "This is the ultimate meanness. I think we should get rid of her and take over the farm."

"And free all the other animals too," said Mary.

"Yeah," said Pee Wee. "Then it'll be our farm. We can change the name and everything."

"To what?"

"I don't know, how about Rodent Farm?"

Snip of the Tale: An indirect reference. When allusions are made to other works or events we recognize, it enhances our reading pleasure. Here the allusion is to *Animal Farm*, by George Orwell. The allusion above is also an example of intertextuality.

ARCHETYPE

THE OLD BEARDED MOUSE

THE HAG MOUSE

THE GREAT MOTHER MOUSE

VILLAGE IDIOT MOUSE

Snip of the Tale: The original on which copies are modeled. Archetypes have a deep, ingrained appeal for us; nevertheless, we like them to have some quirks and idiosyncrasies when they turn up on the page.

OXYMORON

It was a slow run that caused the mice to lose their tails.
It was a dull knife that caused their soundless wails.

Snip of the Tale: Contradictory language. "Oxymoron" comes from the Greek *oxys*, "sharp, keen," and *mōros*, "dull, foolish."

STRUCTURE
EXAMPLES BROUGHT TO YOU BY THE *TTT THESAURUS*

For the architect: blueprints to give you the overall design

For the wedding planner: endless details that make the big event come off

For the conductor: orchestrating the symphony to make harmony

For the builder: foundation, beams, and framework

For the halfway handyman: glue and chewed bubble gum

For the writer: all of the above and more

Snip of the Tale: How a work is organized. Stories within a work can be told by alternating characters. Works can be thematically or topically structured, and many outside patterns (both man-made and in nature) can be used as structural devices.

Tale according to Oscar: relates some event, real or imagined.

Tale according to Mary: is similar to short story, although it is a somewhat broader term; for example, a scary story or a folktale.

Tail according to Pee Wee: "is what we don't have anymore."

Snip of the Tale: A brief narrative.

SHORT SHORT **STORY**

Woman wields knife; three tailless mice.

Snip of the Tale: Story with few words.

CHARACTER

A person trapped in a story that seems like a real human being.

"Hey, wait a minute. What about mice? What about hobbits and fairies and unicorns and white rabbits? And you better include some intergalactic dudes."

Hmm. A creature trapped in a story that seems like a real human being.

"Seems human!" Pee Wee's hand went automatically to the stub on his rump. "I would never cut off a person's appendage."

"I would," said Oscar. "You bet."

"I might," said Mary, "depending on the circumstances."

Hmm. A creature trapped in a story that seems like a real human being—i.e., moral constitution.

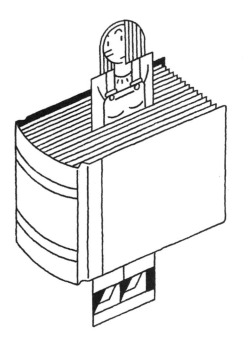

Snip of the Tale: Generally based on the moral makeup of human personality and behavior.

CHARACTER PRESENTATION (INDIRECT METHOD)

Pee Wee is the youngest and sometimes thinks the world revolves around him. He loves to nibble on pink erasers. Secretly, he wants to be a writer and is working on a book called *It's Such a Hard Life*. The toaster is his favorite appliance to play in. His faults include stealing shiny things and hoarding them like a dragon.

Mary is the oldest survivor and big sister. She has to intervene when Oscar and Pee Wee fight. Her favorite hobby is reading; she's a know-it-all, but not in a showy way. She's amazingly calm under pressure. Thanks to her, no one bled to death when their tails were lopped off. Her faults include trying to be too good, which is exhausting for everyone.

Oscar is famous for hurling Shakespearean insults like ninja *shuriken*. Next to the Bard, his favorite thing to read is Spider-Man comics. He loves his whiskers and slicks them down to form a Fu Manchu mustache. The female Mus dig him! He's terribly conceited, although he's very insecure about his buckteeth and the head scar where an electrode was implanted. His faults include not being very nice to his sister and brother, and occasionally playing with fire.

Snip of the Tale: How an author presents her characters to the reader. The method above is sometimes referred to as authorial interpretation because the author is telling you what to think.

CHARACTER PRESENTATION (DIRECT METHOD)

"Hey, who ate my fly?" Pee Wee looked from Oscar to Mary and back again.

Mary cleared her throat and continued reading. "Not I."

"Somebody did. All that's left are these stupid wings which are as tasteless as church mice wafers." His nose twitched and his ears were getting redder by the minute. "I know it was you, Oscar."

"It was getting stale on the windowsill."

Pee Wee threw one of the wings at Oscar and made him lose count of the matchsticks in the booklet he had found. "Nuh-uh. I was waiting for it to get crunchy."

"Give me a break. It was practically mummified when we got here."

"That was my fly. You and Mary ate yours already, and that one was mine." He threw the other wing. It clipped Oscar in the eye, and soon the two were biting and clawing each other. Mary let it go on for a minute before she separated them.

Oscar put a hand to his neck. "You bit me, like, twenty times."

"I'll bite you some more," said Pee Wee. He lunged, but Mary held him back. Spit was coming out of his snout, and a vein in his neck was throbbing. Pee Wee carried on like a rabid fool, but inside he was chilling. After all, it was a bluebottle fly—which was pretty but didn't taste nearly as good as the common housefly. But it would be totally uncool to pretend like he didn't care, because after all, it was his, and what if it *had* been one of his favorite varieties?

$\int nip$ of the $Tale:$ How an author presents her characters to the reader. The method above is called direct because it uses appearance, action, speech and thought to present the characters directly to the reader.

NARRATOR
BAR NONE

THE ONE WHO TELLS THE STORY

"Me," said Pee Wee, "I'm the narrator."
"No," said Mary, "we're all taking turns."

Snip of the Tale: There are many combinations and types of narrators— reliable or unreliable, frame, objective, I, we, you, omniscient, or a narrator loosely disguised as the author—but essentially it comes down to who tells the story.

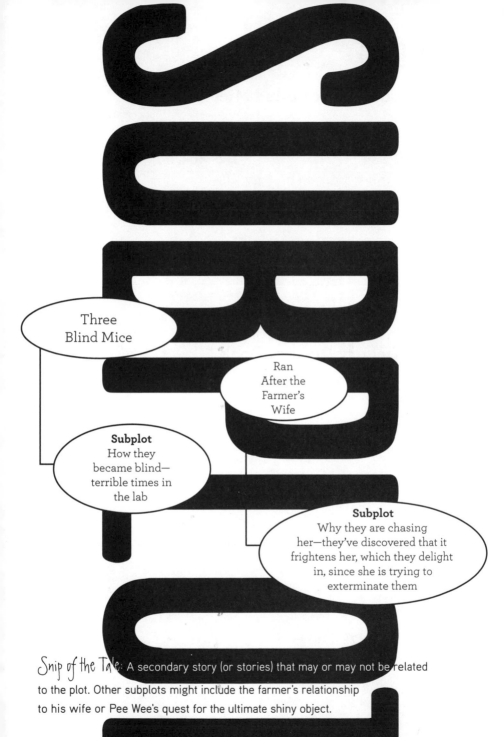

SUBPLOT

Three Blind Mice

Ran After the Farmer's Wife

Subplot
How they became blind—terrible times in the lab

Subplot
Why they are chasing her—they've discovered that it frightens her, which they delight in, since she is trying to exterminate them

Snip of the Tale: A secondary story (or stories) that may or may not be related to the plot. Other subplots might include the farmer's relationship to his wife or Pee Wee's quest for the ultimate shiny object.

GROTESQUE

Grotesque: Three Blind Mice

Three blind mice,
See how they run,
A farmer married an ugly wife,
And she cut her throat with a carving knife,
Did you ever see such a fool in your life,
Three blind mice.

(This variant of the rhyme is from the 1800s or perhaps earlier.)

Not: Hickory Dickory Dock

Hickory dickory dock,
The mouse ran up the clock,
The clock struck one,
The mouse ran down;
Hickory dickory dock.

Snip of the Tale: This refers to characters (and events) that are bizarre, incongruous, and abnormal. The grotesque is not limited to the physical; spiritual and psychological ugliness graze on this terrain as well.

SCIENCE FICTION
THE MICE MEET SPAMDROIDS

Pee Wee blinked. "Where are we? This looks like a lab."

"And how did we get here?" asked Mary.

"We were standing by that rock after the meteor shower," said Oscar.

Just then the door opened and in came a dozen mice, one as beautiful as the next.

Oscar licked his snout. "This place suddenly got more appealing."

Mary noticed a red light coming from their eyes. "These are just machines covered in mouse fur."

The leader spoke: "We've brought you here to give you what you couldn't give yourselves—tails. We've the technology to grow them."

"What's the catch?" asked Mary. "And why don't any of *you* have tails?"

"We're Spamdroids and thus have no need of them."

Before Mary could inquire further, Pee Wee began hopping around the room. "I want, want, want my tail back, right now!"

Some days later they were miserable beyond imagining. Pee Wee's tail was an intelligent design, all right. It constantly tried to drag him backward, as if *he* were the tail. Mary's plight was no better. Her tail had gotten so long that she'd taken to rolling it like yarn. Meanwhile, Oscar's tail kept mutating, until he had several stemming from the same root. "If we have to," said Oscar, "we'll chop them off ourselves."

Snip of the Tale: Fantasy pertaining to speculative scientific/technological discovery and its impact on society or an individual. Takes place in a different time and/or space.

HUMORS
TAKE THE OLD-FASHIONED PERSONALITY TEST

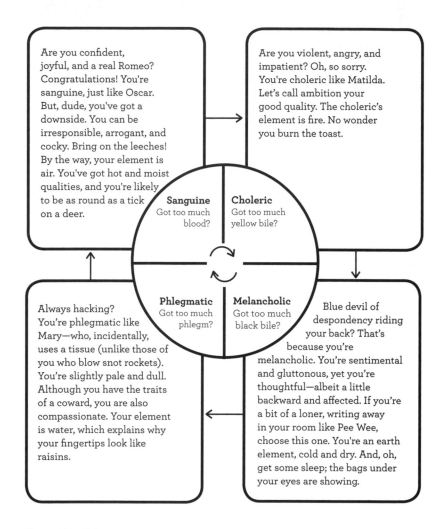

Are you confident, joyful, and a real Romeo? Congratulations! You're sanguine, just like Oscar. But, dude, you've got a downside. You can be irresponsible, arrogant, and cocky. Bring on the leeches! By the way, your element is air. You've got hot and moist qualities, and you're likely to be as round as a tick on a deer.

Are you violent, angry, and impatient? Oh, so sorry. You're choleric like Matilda. Let's call ambition your good quality. The choleric's element is fire. No wonder you burn the toast.

Sanguine
Got too much blood?

Choleric
Got too much yellow bile?

Phlegmatic
Got too much phlegm?

Melancholic
Got too much black bile?

Always hacking? You're phlegmatic like Mary—who, incidentally, uses a tissue (unlike those of you who blow snot rockets). You're slightly pale and dull. Although you have the traits of a coward, you are also compassionate. Your element is water, which explains why your fingertips look like raisins.

Blue devil of despondency riding your back? That's because you're melancholic. You're sentimental and gluttonous, yet you're thoughtful—albeit a little backward and affected. If you're a bit of a loner, writing away in your room like Pee Wee, choose this one. You're an earth element, cold and dry. And, oh, get some sleep; the bags under your eyes are showing.

Snip of the Tale: Way back, the body's four liquids (blood, yellow bile, phlegm, and black bile) were called humors. This medical classification expanded over time to include temperament, and humors became mankind's first attempt to classify personality. The best Elizabethan characters in Shakespeare's day were those whose humors had run awry.

TRAGEDY

She cut off their tails with a carving knife.

Snip of the Tale: Over the years the meaning of this term has varied widely, but quintessentially it's misfortune and calamity that play out on the page or stage.

EPILOGUE

Pee Wee went on to write his story, which became an instant bestseller.

Oscar continues to romance Pee Wee's publicist, makeup artist, personal assistant, as well as every other female mouse with a little twitching snout. Occasionally he will slap Pee Wee in the back of the head, but less so now that Pee Wee bankrolls his enterprises and adventures.

Mary met the mouse of her dreams, and together they opened a peanut stand. To date there are forty-three stores specializing in peanut brittle.

Matilda Bethoon continues to be a miceanthrope and set traps.

Snip of the Tale: Life after the story ends, like bell-bottoms, may be out of fashion but probably not for too long. The word itself may be omitted, but check out the last chapter of current novels and you'll find some reemerging fashions.

TOUR DE FORCE

A mouse that writes a bestselling book riffing off a nursery rhyme.

Snip of the Tale: A show of skill.

INTRODUCTION, PREFACE, FOREWORD

$\mathcal{S}$nip of the Tale: Introduction, preface, and foreword are all parts of a book's front matter, that which comes before the actual body of the text. Some sources claim these three terms are virtually interchangeable; others not. At times like these, why not love a prologue written by the author/narrator/character?

ACKNOWLEDGMENTS

I am indebted to my mother for all the nursery rhymes she taught me as a child; to my editor extraordinaire Caitlyn Dlouhy; to designer Debra Sfetsios-Conover for helping to make this book look so terrific; to Jeannie Ng for making sure the mice behaved themselves grammatically; to writers, like Jerome Stern and Janet Burroway, who taught me; to Beauvais McCaddon, whose enthusiasm for the early drafts of this work gave me courage; to Naomi Holoch, who read final drafts and offered commentary; to Raymond Queneau's *Exercises in Style*; to the well-worn copy of Holman and Harmon's *A Handbook to Literature* from my graduate-school days; to E. M. Forster's *Aspects of the Novel*; to *The Paris Review*'s writers' interviews; to essays by Gertrude Stein and John Ruskin; and to so many unnamed others . . . thank you.

—C. L.

For those who want more detail than the Snips of the Tales, this appendix is for you.

APPENDIX

Allegory (p. 32): An allegory is a story meant to be read on two levels, the most obvious being the characters and situation at hand, and the other, what they represent as an extended metaphor. In the example, the sponge is named Compassion, a fairly obvious clue, while the knife's representation is a little less clear-cut (at least until the end). This is an ancient form, and you spelunkers out there might want to check out Plato's "Allegory of the Cave." John Bunyan's *Pilgrim's Progress* is another classic example of this form, but perhaps more familiar to today's readers would be *The Lion, the Witch and the Wardrobe* by C. S. Lewis or Antoine de Saint-Exupéry's wonderful story of *The Little Prince*.

Allusion (p. 100): Whereas a reference is specific, an allusion tends to be more indirect. For effectiveness, an allusion depends upon a reader's prior knowledge and sensibilities. Let's say a quarreling couple wants to sort out their disagreements, and they agree to meet at a local Greek diner, Thermopylae. Knowing that Thermopylae is the site of a famous battle in ancient Greece leads the reader to suspect that the attempted reconciliation at the diner may not turn out so well. To those who don't get the reference, it's just the name of another Greek diner. Complex literary allusion is often essential to our understanding of fine writing. It can enhance a work and enrich our appreciation on a deeper level by evoking associations of an event, work, person, or object of which we have prior knowledge. However, too many abstruse allusions in your work may become lost to the reader. Are they really allusions? (If a tree falls in the forest . . .) By comparing your work to other great works, you, in some ways, hold yourself up to the standard of that work. You may get noticed, but it may not be the kind of notice you want, either.

Ambiguity (p. 96): The difference between an ambiguous ending and a confusing one can mean the difference between an artistic rendering and an amateurish one. Ambiguous endings leave the reader pondering more than one outcome. We're torn between two possible truths. In the John Fowles novel *The French Lieutenant's Woman*, the author (turned character) discusses his plot dilemma and then writes different but equally plausible endings. We're left to vacillate between possible truths and, in so doing, come closer to attaining a truth than if we had been told outright. Ambiguity can also function on a much smaller scale. Some words can have antithetical meanings, as in Pee Wee's double Dutch examples. Playing with such words, as well as exploiting the delightfully rich sentence structure of our language, can take one to new heights. A politician delivered one of my all-time favorite sentences of syntactic ambiguity. Following a local flood he said: "This is the worst disaster in California since I was elected."

Archetype (p. 101): An archetype is an original model or prototype upon which other things are copied or patterned. Today, one can hardly talk about archetype without the name of Carl Jung surfacing. In the "collective unconscious" Jung proposed, there are primordial images we all share. We are attracted to stories that present these deeply imbedded patterns of thought or images. Effective writers know that even Father Zeus or Mother Earth figures need some individual traits and eccentricities if they are to appeal to readers on more than one level.

Avant-Garde (p. 13): This type of artist is a bit like an oppositional adolescent who challenges everything: difficult and unpredictable (and let's not forget messy). They do, however, pave the way, so for the siblings who follow, life is not quite as difficult. Gertrude Stein's experiments with language put her in this category. She, like other writers of her generation, chipped away at ideas of art. In the example, the reader, like the mice, must also work her way through the maze of text that at times runs contrary to expectation. This requires some effort on the part of the reader—as does the form in general. If you've never taken a look at *Calligrammes* by the French poet Guillaume Apollinaire, treat yourself. Poets in particular have long played with the spacing of words on a page. Nowhere does this seem more evident than in concrete poetry. Among other things, such poems make use of spaces, symbols, and colors. If onomatopoeias use words that suggest their meaning by sound, what about words whose shape on the page (like "hop" in the example) visually reinforces or defines their meaning (or perhaps the words take a shape that has nothing to do with the meaning we assign to them)? The work itself may become a collage, a blending of text, lines, and images. With computer graphics, fonts, and clip art, the only limit is your own imagination. Warning: not many may understand you or what you're trying to do, but at your age, that should come as no surprise.

Beginnings (p. 78): You can't judge a book by its cover, but a reader will often judge your story by its beginning. And although it may sound harsh, Oscar (that dirty rat) tells me he never reads a book beyond the first paragraph unless it grabs him by the whiskers. So, time spent on a beginning is worth the effort. Frustratingly, you may write a hundred beginnings before you have your first "true" beginning. And you may not find this true beginning until you reach the end. And if at the end you find a problem with the ending, look for the solution in the beginning.

Bildungsroman (p. 88): Although purists may cite a technical objection or two between this and the coming-of-age novel (bildungsromans, for example, have autobiographical roots), they both essentially deal with the maturation of a young protagonist. *To Kill a Mockingbird*, *Great Expectations*, Harry Potter, *The Reader*, and *The Adventures of Huckleberry Finn* all fall into this category. There are some masterful short stories as well that deal with adolescent angst. Among them are Richard McCann's *My Mother's Clothes: The School of Beauty and Shame* and Carson McCullers's *Wunderkind*.

Catharsis (p. 99): Historically, this term has both religious and medical applications, but one can hardly talk about catharsis without referring to Aristotle, who discussed it in relation to tragedy in the *Poetics*. Catharsis essentially means purging. (Did he intend the purging to mean plot complications or emotions? Hmm.) What is clear is that, for the audience, an emotional cleansing is likely to take place. Ever leave the tragic ending of a show feeling exhilarated and wonder what that's about? Consult the work of this Greek genius for further information.

Cause and Effect (p. 14): Puzzle pieces are not interchangeable. Each has a specific place and connection to those adjoining it; together they make a whole and thus present a unified picture. If a piece is missing or a connection forced, the whole picture appears less complete and satisfying. In some ways cause and effect can be thought of as pieces to a puzzle whose interlinking is essential to plot. In the example, the linkage goes like this: torture led to escape, escape to freedom, freedom provided opportunity for retaliation, retaliation fueled destruction, destruction brought accusations of arson and resulted in nonpayment, nonpayment triggered bankruptcy, bankruptcy signaled an end to laboratory testing. Bingo!

Character (p. 106): Whether hobbit, human, or mouse, our concept of character is generally based on human personality and its moral makeup. The mice felt the subject of character was worth four chapters: first, trying to define what is meant by character. Then addressing the challenge that writers must face when presenting a character on the page. There are direct (when the author does the telling) and indirect methods (appearance, action, speech, and thought) of presenting a character. There are also round and flat characters—distinctions made by E. M. Forster in his enduring *Aspects of the Novel*. Of course, the mice could go on and on, but someone had to stop them. . . .

Cliché (p. 58): Something new under the sun? You bet, if the writer is fresh in her treatment and combination of story, situation, and language. By changing the angle of the light and shade, you affect the entire viewing. Your readers may recognize the same old expression and subject matter, but they will be made to *feel* the energy of something new and original in your carefully arranged composition. Look: "kick the bucket" can morph into "clicked the bucket," exemplifying that writers familiar with clichés have the advantage of flipping them for various effects. This is lost on the less evolved writer who thinks her expression is original. And indeed it was—when it first appeared on the cave walls of Lascaux. So you need to figure out what is cliché and what is not. As a writer it's part of the evolutionary path you must follow if you are to compete and survive in the world. But do not shun a cliché. Begin by trying to understand it and its function. See it as something that is powerful enough to bind the living and the dead. But first you might begin by examining the word. Here's a brief etymological digression: the word "cliché" itself (past participle of the French verb *"clicher"* meaning "to stereotype," and further back from the old French *"cliquer,"* meaning "to click") evolved from printers' jargon. After scores of printings, stereotype plates—used to make reproductions—wear down. Along the way, the term was extended to an idea or expression that is commonplace, hackneyed, or trite. Simply, worn out from use.

Coincidence (p. 53): Historically, coincidence has been a staple device of plot. Although novels per se didn't exist in Aristotle's day, writers later borrowed elements from Greek dramas to tell their stories. Say two characters (Oedipus and Laius) happen to be in the same place (a juncture of roads), and what ensues is significant to one or both (Oedipus kills Laius). Aristotle would consider this coincidence as fate. With the sudden turn of events the character realizes the full impact of his actions (I'm married to Mom and I've killed Dad) and kills himself. Who could ask for a better tragedy? We are horrified, fascinated, and moved to pity. Aristotle notes that when chance events happen for a purpose (i.e., causal connection), they seem most astonishing to the audience. Now, consider the much beloved Dickens. If it weren't for coincidence, his novels would lack plot. Before modern readers start pooh-poohing his Victorian sensibilities, let's remember that his books are still in print and that his characters—with deferred recognition and family reunion scenes—still captivate modern readers, despite the deus ex machina contrivances and outlandish coincidences that salt the page. Just ask Pip, Nell, or Oliver. Conversely, the post-post-modern writer will be the first to yell horse-hockey and then toss chance with causality out the window and declare that everything is random. Things no longer happen for a reason, and if coincidence occurs, it just does. Better yet, coincidence takes place in the mind of the reader. Here's an example: a favorite rhyme of a traveling storyteller is about the three blind mice. He has a habit of telling versions of this story while at the local bar drinking Bloody Marys and flicking his lighter. The mice may never figure out a connection to this example, but you might, dear reader, if you continue reading. Then again, perhaps you won't because there is none. As reader and writer, you must make up your own mind about coincidence and probabilities in fiction. Certain story forms, like the road trip or the journey, lend themselves to chance happenings. How much coincidence is too much before it seems forced or even farcical? Check out the improbabilities in the song "I'm My Own Grandpa" by Moe Jaffe and Dwight Latham.

Denouement (p. 89): This literally is an unknotting (from the French *"dénouer,"* "to untie"). In fiction, it refers to the part of the story where the plot complications are undone. In the classic mystery, the denouement would be the part where Holmes explains to Watson (and thus to us as readers) how the murderer went about the crime. In essence, all the twists and turns connected to the plot are straightened out: villains are identified, those separated by misfortune or other circumstances are reunited, etc. Denouement is sometimes thought of as falling action; the crisis has already occurred and the story is moving toward a resolution. Along the way (and often rather rapidly in contemporary fiction), whatever loose ends remain are cleared up (or left perhaps ambiguously satisfying) and the story ends. Books on plot are plentiful. A century ago, Georges Polti wrote *The Thirty-Six Dramatic Situations*. Still others insist there are more and less plot situations than this.

Description (p. 62): The Greeks counted description among the major types of composition. Description helps the reader to picture the setting and to visualize the characters and the scene as it unfolds. Imagine a battle at sea where there's no description. How long would you keep reading? When your reader tastes the salt air on her tongue and squints when eyeing the bright waves, you're underway. But how much description is enough? Shape and surface complexion aside, what else can you say about a nose? What does the area around it look like—freckled, tanned, caked with eczema? Much ado has been made about the wart on the Miller's nose in Chaucer's *Canterbury Tales*, with its protruding tuft of hair, red as the bristles of a sow's ears. Chaucer well knew the power of one vivid detail to sum up a character. The caricaturist David Levine exaggerated the outstanding features of his subjects when he drew them. A writer too must translate the important features of her characters into words and, unless intended, avoid caricature.

Description that is often blended into the story seems to be the going norm these days, although some of us still long for the long passages of description that writers like Balzac can serve up.

Detail (p. 70): Concrete details appeal to the senses; often through them readers are led to ideas and judgments and thus ultimately to larger moral conclusions. In the novel *Abeng*, if Michelle Cliff had written: "Colonialism has profited from exploiting Jamaicans and exporting their citrus, cane, and bananas. But mangoes are the one thing we won't let you take from us," we might as well be reading an essay. Instead, in the opening pages, she takes us on an excursion of the senses, where we see the yellow and gold fibers of the mango, feel its stringy consistency as the hairlike fibers close to the seed tighten around our teeth. Our mouth burns from the sap and tingles from the juice. We taste, too, the difference between the two mangoes, the common and the St. Julienne. Because the writing is colorful and precise, we are active participants in what is taking place. Through these images we are able to draw conclusions and make generalizations without being told.

Deus ex Machina (p. 85): Here's another term that has its roots in ancient Greek drama. When the gods or god ("deus") graced the stage, it was usually by way of some contraptionlike machine ("machina") that lowered them from above. It was a good indication that the character had no humanly way possible out of the predicament s/he was facing except through divine intervention. Because any such resolution does not arise organically out of the story, Aristotle criticized its application in serious drama. In fiction, the term is slapped on any unlikely surprise or coincidence that the writer artificially inserts in the story. Often such contrivances lead to happy endings and/or punishment of villainous characters. Fear not if you favor such devices; one writer's trash is another's pleasure. If serious fiction pooh-poohs deus ex machina, comedy and farce welcome it.

Dialect (p. 71): Isolation gave birth to dialects. In today's connected world, not only are the number of languages disappearing, so too are dialects. Although not as ubiquitous, or perhaps as regionally distinct as a hundred years ago, robust dialects still flourish. When writing, think of dialect as a spice. You need just a little for flavor. Add too much, and no matter how good the other ingredients of your story may be, you're likely to ruin it. You want to keep your misspellings at a minimum too. Your readers are not cryptologists. Notice that syntax and word choice help to characterize and make dialect easier on the eyes than beaucoo mizpelings.

Dialogue (p. 21): Dialogue that is individuated, tension filled, immediate, and economically tagged grabs the reader's attention for the same reason that it's more interesting to watch a juggler with an assortment of knives as opposed to one juggling two tennis balls. The scene makes use of gestures, too—Pee Wee's paw chewing, Mary's necklace tugging. A scene built on dialogue that reveals and develops character and situation is sure to be memorable to the reader. Suspense is building in the example, too. Is Oscar's plan dangerous? Will it succeed? Questions raised in the mind of the reader actively involve her, and she'll keep reading. A word about speech tags: When you need them, "he said" or "she said" will do nicely. And a word about tics: If your characters stutter or stammer, an "um" or two will suffice; you don't need every Ooh Eeh Ooh Ah Aah Ting Tang Walla Walla Bing Bang.

Diction (p. 74): Do you say "potato" or "spud"? "Sentimental" or "cheesy"? Are your word choices simple or multisyllabic? Are you choosing glittering words because they sound pretty or do you shun the fool's gold and go for the occasional gold nugget? How, too, the words are strung together can be a matter of diction.

Epigram (p. 33): Included in the examples given is a two-line epigram on immortality. Along with the mice theme, it plays off *Moby-Dick* and puns Oscar Wilde, who was well known for quips of this form, by using Oscar's name as author. Contemporary devotees who have made use of epigrams in their work include poets Robert Frost and John Hollander and the writer Dorothy Parker, who was famous for droll utterances. If you're witty and brief, try writing stand-up comedy, fortune cookies, or obituaries for papers of questionable merit.

Epilogue (p. 116): This is what happens after the story ends. *The World According to Garp* by John Irving is followed by an epilogue entitled "Life after Garp," in which we learn what happened to many of the main characters we came to care about in the novel. While "epilogue" may be fashionably omitted today, like the blind cc (carbon copy) of an e-mail we often are still privy to what unfolds.

Epistolary Novel (p. 72): The epistolary novel dates to the mid-sixteenth century. By the 1700s, Fanny Burney and Samuel Richardson brought the form to a popular pinnacle. In contemporary fiction, this form has met with waning success, an exception being Alice Walker's *The Color Purple*, in which the young narrator, Celie, writes letters to God.

Today, letter writing seems more like a lost art than a part of daily life. As e-mail, text messages, tweets, and other fragmented forms of communication insinuate themselves into our lives, they are apt to appear with greater frequency in stories and novels. Like other various insertions, they can add variety to a work. They may even make the reader LOL. It's not such a far stretch to imagine that the epistolary form may reinvent itself by way of text messaging.

Exposition (p. 81): There are numerous ways of handling expository information. There's nothing wrong with a straightforward approach—time, place, and character, laid out like flatware. You can sling it all in one heaping spoonful like shepherd's pie—but how appetizing is that compared to a ten-course meal that arrives gradually over the course of the evening, tantalizing tidbits to whet your appetite and keep you going as you wait for the next morsel in this literary feast. There's nothing on the plate that isn't edible.

F_ _K (p. 38): If "feck," "fink," "flak," "folk," "fork," "funk" will do,
Why invoke "F _ _ K" unless you need to?

Fable and Parable (pp. 90–91): That these ancient forms endure is a testament to their power. Despite their longevity, it would be folly to think that all possible subject matters have been exhausted. The modern fabulist lives in a ripe junkyard of material. Franz Kafka, George Orwell, and James Thurber have all nosed around in there and harvested matter. Because forms like fable, parable, and allegory can often be read and interpreted on multiple levels, they offer special appeal for those writers who might wish to speak to both children and adults, or to the child within the adult. The writer's style here becomes particularly important.

Fairy Tale (p. 34): Here, the classic elements of fairy tale are illustrated (undefined place and time; unchanged/undeveloped characters; a prohibition that affects plot; magic and transformation) as the mice seek refuge from the impending winter in the forest. Any serious student of folklore will tell you there's a lot more to these stories than just the stories themselves. They're ubiquitous; they cross cultural boundaries and resonate in interior landscapes as dim as the unconscious. (Take a look at Bruno Bettelheim's *The Uses of Enchantment*, and Aladdin's lamp will take on a whole new meaning.) Forms that emerge from the populous, like folk and fairy tales, are not only fun, they're instructive.

Hybrid possibilities are out there. Can you think of an ogre who is not only the main character of a story but also its hero? Why does this new prince charming resonate with so many?

Farce (p. 36): This form of comedy has popular appeal. It relies on humor to exploit a situation instead of using character development to move a plot forward. Bad puns, caricatures, jokes, sexual innuendos, and slapstick from a vaudevillian past abound in this scene. One can see the migration pattern from the old-world theatrical tradition to the new world of TV sitcoms, where farce seems now to mostly reside. In farce of both stage and screen, the artifice of deus ex machina is often employed as a plot device.

Flashback (p. 52): Although a flashback is useful in developing a character more fully, a protracted flashback can undercut a story's momentum. Notice how sensory triggers (what one character hears, sees, touches, etc.) can become smooth passages into the internal landscape. For example, your character passes a street vendor selling roasted chestnuts, and the smell transports him back to childhood, when his mother stopped at a stand and bought him a brown sack full of the treasures, he was shocked to find the taste medicinal. . . .

Foreshadowing (p. 29): There's an old joke about a man who returns from vacation and his neighbor tells him that his cat is dead. The man says to his neighbor, "That's no way to tell me such a thing. You have to prepare me; for example, you begin by saying you first noticed my cat on the roof . . ." In the same way, foreshadowing prepares the reader for events that later unfold in the story. At the time, these things may not seem obvious, but in looking back, the signs are there. Foreshadowing can take many forms: choice of objects, repetition, character traits, etc.

Formula (p. 54): For many this term connotes writing that lacks innovation because it uses recycled plots and ideas without adding anything fresh to the recipe. Perhaps closer to the truth: Formulas are a staple of writing, and by using different proportions and combinations, a good writer, like a good chef, does come up with something delicious and appealing. Consider, for example, what Frank Herbert added to the lore of the spice trade by writing *Dune*, a novel set in the future in which the priceless spice mélange triples life expectancy. Try out formulas the way Ruth Wakefield did in 1930 when improvising led to chocolate chip cookies. Don't be afraid to experiment. It was a St. Louis doctor who, in 1890, turned peanuts into peanut butter, and later, in 1932, when Rosefield added chunks of peanuts for a crunchy effect. Give yourself permission to play—like the gambling earl of Sandwich who brought us meat between two slices of bread some three hundred years ago. Variations have been sprouting ever since. If experimenting with formulas, ask yourself questions. Must a Western have cowboys and horses? Must a mystery involve a murder? And how about combining formulas: Could a detective story be set on Mars?

Frame Story (p. 69): Just as the inspiration for the Russian doll came from Japan, the frame story, too, traveled from east to the west. Organizing a main story, which contains many lesser stories within it, is an ancient and clichéd form of storytelling. Oscar's examples are older and not as psychologically complex as Mary's examples, in which the main narrator is somehow affected by the story s/he narrates. In single frame stories, the reliability of the narrator is sometimes called into question. None of this mattered to Oscar; he particularly admired the Boccacio tale about a grieving woman who secretly kept her lover's head in a basil pot as well as Christine de Pizan's tale about the woman who nursed her own mother while in prison. (Sometimes there will even be a story within a story whose subject matter sums up or comments on the outer frame [known as *mise en abîme*].) Lastly, Pee Wee's example of framing his younger self, experiences, and stories within the more mature self allows him a certain distance and reflection, yet immediacy can be gained when he evokes the inner child and slides into that child's world and viewpoint. Nitpickers would not consider Pee Wee's story a frame narrative if the outer frame (the mature self) takes more of the spotlight. But the thing to think about, dear reader, is whether the frame is necessary at all for your storytelling purposes. You figure this out, of course, by experimenting on your own and by looking at how others have used this form.

Grotesque (p. 112): If it's ugly or abnormal, fantastic or creepy, it's likely to be called grotesque. Works by Edgar Allen Poe come to mind. The grotesque refers not only to subject matter but to characters, and not just to their physical abnormalities—there're spiritual and psychological deformities as well. Sherwood Anderson is among those who have written in this vein with piercing clarity. *Winesburg, Ohio* is brilliant, and Anderson's work merits greater recognition than it has received. Other terrific writers who've courted the grotesque include Flannery O'Connor and Eudora Welty. O'Connor is especially dark. Good lord, bring a flashlight with you.

Hero (Not) (p. 60): In the past, traditional heroes were nothing short of godlike. If they had a weakness, it was likely to be a single unfortunate trait (hubris, for example) that led to their downfall. Today's protagonist may have more flaws than a pack of socks bought at a street fair. Once you get into the package you discover loose threads, dye irregularities, mismatched sizes, and my god—a pair of toe socks for six toes. But you are attracted to their color, and the cotton is oh so soft. And although you are loathe to admit it—your left foot is a half size smaller than your right—those mismatched socks are not so far removed from your own foot. Over time you develop an affinity for this odd lot of socks. Even with their many flaws they seem more interesting and feel more natural to you than the static spandex varieties. They're slightly grotesque but intriguing. They give your feet a kind of character that traditional—and perfect—socks lack.

Humors (p. 114): You might think of humors as the first personality classification. There have been a plethora since this early model and there will undoubtedly be more in the future.

Fear of pigeonholing personalities according to humors didn't stop Shakespeare or other Elizabethan playwrights from taking full advantage of popular conceptions to help explain their characters' bizarre behaviors.

Immediacy (p. 5): Whack your funny bone, and there is no escaping the sensation. The response is immediate. A skillful writer can trigger a similar sense of immediacy, where the reader feels she is right there as events unfold. Dialogue, action, and description are all contributing factors. The sense of immediacy is often heightened by the use of the present tense.

Insertion (p. 30): I was captivated by the many insertions in Max Frisch's *Man in the Holocene*. The work simply wouldn't be what it is without them. Inserting what may at first appear to be odd or extraneous material into a text can indeed add depth, variety, and interest to fiction. One need only look at Laurence Sterne's *The Life and Times of Tristram Shandy*, as Pee Wee clearly did before drawing line squiggles of his own tail. In addition to the standard diary, letter, and journal entry that have filled the pages of fiction past, new possibilities have evolved due to technology: text messages, tweets, e-mails, and chat-room conversations. Regardless of type, these must be insertions that *matter*. Notice that Oscar's Christmas list tells the reader a lot about him: He's a wisecracker ("Hey, Fat Red Man") who's sharp (can distinguish between fake and real diamonds as well as the curing process of pistachios). He has specific interests (magic, verbal jousting) as well as an abnormal interest in fire. These all speak to character and hint at the possibility of a heated scene or two.

Interior Monologue (p. 22): In the late 1800s Édouard Dujardin championed the use of interior monologue in *Les Lauriers sont coupés*. An interior monologue attempts to convey the character's thoughts and emotions in a direct manner. Although the mind is rarely as tidy as it is portrayed when using this technique, the reader does gain a more intimate knowledge and understanding of the character. When coherence and syntax break down, we often refer to this as stream of consciousness.

Intertextuality (p. 40): Many theorists believe that intertextuality is at the core of literature and that every text is built by weaving, transforming, and absorbing other texts. At the root of this is the assumption that writers are readers, and I quite like the idea posited by E. M. Forster of thinking about writers from all historical ages sitting together around a table. You may find you have more in common with a writer who lived a hundred years ago or more than you do with anyone whose current work you are reading. Pull up a chair.

Introduction, Preface, Foreword (p. 118): *See Prologue.*

Irony (p. 96): Most simply, a reality that proves to be different from appearance. The second example on page 96 is a bit subtler, suggesting perhaps there is security in bondage and/or forms of enslavement in freedom. Irony may also be verbal (as in the first example), in which the opposite of what is said is intended. If you're among those who find yourself lost in the misty woods of verbal irony and sarcasm, it's no wonder. Sarcasm can, and does, incorporate verbal irony, and verbal irony can be sarcastic. Here's a bread crumb: Sarcasm is personal and critical, and there is an element of ridicule in sarcasm that is often lacking in verbal irony.

Keyboard Digression (p. 41): Even when the writer is at play, the mice are never far.
There's a wonderful digression in the *Odyssey* that begins soon after Euryclea beholds Odysseus's leg. (I'd love to see a modern keyboard digression of that.) What story can you tell, using only the keyboard? Send it to me.

Legend (p. 16): Early on, legends were concerned with lives of saints, but nowadays legends tend to be connected to a historical place, person, or subject. Collectively, such stories tell us something about a people. Here, the legend is urban, more akin to those collected by folklorist Jan Harold Brunvand in tales like *The Choking Doberman*. Where legends are concerned, readers give more leeway—"all right, so Rip Van Winkle sleeps for years, tell us what happens when he wakes"—but the fiction must still resonate with the audience, and it helps if the writer keeps her distance. A writer can provoke a plethora of reactions from a reading audience by tapping into contemporary fears. By now, Upton Sinclair's *The Jungle*, with its graphic descriptions of the meatpacking industry's unsanitary conditions, has become part of our collective unconscious; so much of urban lore now revolves around the question: "What is really in your fast food?"

Leitmotif (p. 12): In addition to the reoccurrence of an image, object, or action in literature, a story's leitmotif may also be identified by the repetition of certain words or phrases. In the example, I am also playing off the French word *"motif,"* from which "leitmotif" is derived, as it is used in music, referring to a striking rhythm or repetition. Here, it is the chopping of vegetables that foreshadows the triple caudectomy.

Mechanics (p. 27): Imagine driving without agreed-upon road signs. Now imagine that's your writing without proper punctuation. Just a wreck. If you don't know your colon from your period, then you've really put your writing and your *. However, there may be times when you'd rather go off-road. Pay attention to your surroundings. For those of you looking for on-the-road advice, lift and examine a copy of *The Elements of Style* by Strunk and White. Karen Gordon's *The Well-Tempered Sentence* and *The Transitive Vampire* offer some sassy bites of advice, too. And with chapters like "Comma Sutra" in Patricia T. O'Conner's *Woe Is I*, you would-be-grammarian autodidacts never had it so good/well.

Metafiction (p. 3): This is illustrated as fiction that consciously comments on itself. For example, premise and suspension of disbelief in relation to the all-important question "How can blind mice see?" is commented upon. Character motivation of the mice is explained as well. The reader learns the mice have some unpleasant connection to laboratory cosmetic experimentation, a lethal product of which they find in Matilda's bathroom.

Mise-en-Scène (p. 94): A dramatic term concerned with the stage setting of a play. This term has also been more broadly applied to film. For writers it can be enormously useful to visualize a scene by drawing it. What furniture is in the room? What's on the walls? Where are the characters in relation to objects and one another? Often what's clear in our own minds doesn't always translate onto the page, and writers are surprised, sometimes annoyed, when readers don't "get it." (Draw a scene after you've written it, sketching only what's mentioned in the text. *That* can be an enlightening exercise.) In the example, Pee Wee is attempting to re-create the farmhouse kitchen—their Eden—before the fall of the knife.

Myth (p. 92): Who are we? Why are we here? How did everything around us come to be as it is? What is our place in the universe? All cultures, ancient and modern, have asked these questions and looked to story, art, philosophy, and the heavens for explanations. Although the answers may no longer be the same as those arrived at by our predecessors, our questioning remains constant. The more you know about mythology, the richer your work is likely to be. Your character stops for cigarettes and gas outside of Allentown, Pennsylvania. He walks out of the convenience store with a book of matches advertising Hephaestus Ironworks. The matches are damp and crooked at the base. Not a single one will light.

Names (p. 11): The Romans believed names were a form of destiny. While there are nameless and memorable characters in fiction—the anti-hero in Dostoyevsky's *Notes from the Underground* being one—names are generally necessary and should be chosen with a poetic care that takes into consideration sound and syllable. Choosing a name that is consonant with the character's milieu and past seems logical. Other good rules of thumb include clarity and simplicity; however, if you *do* want your character to stick out like a sore thumb, pretentious and overly determined names will do the trick. Numerous other factors are examined in the trial and error of this section before all three mice get their names: Mary, Pee Wee, and Oscar. The name of a memorable character can evoke her entire story: Emma Bovary, Clarissa Dalloway. Even single names have power: Gandalf, Alice, Hamlet, Genji, Ahab. A final striking example of the importance of names is that of the cunning Odysseus who saved his life and those of his men by claiming his name was Nobody.

Narrator (p. 110): The narrator is the one telling the story. (Unreliable narrator and point of view are both germane topics worth consulting.) For those who want to learn more about narrators, I suggest making a list of all the narrators from your most favorite books. What do they have in common? Are they resilient? Strong? Intelligent? Afraid sometimes but not too afraid to act? These sorts of examinations will teach you a lot about your preferences as a reader and conversely what kind of narrator you might craft should you try a story of your own. Most of us prefer characters who act, even when they make the wrong decisions. At least they are still attempting to take charge of their lives.

Oxymoron (p. 102): Do I contradict myself? Very well, then. I must be invoking the power of the oxymoron. Combining contradictory words is what an oxymoron is all about. It slows the reader down in a good way, making her think about language, the author's intent and so forth. Some oxymorons have fallen into such common usage that their power as visual speed bumps has all but flattened out. We hardly balk at the incongruity of combinations like "friendly fire," "sour candy," "working lunch," "burning cold," and "alone in a crowd." In a language as alive and rich as ours, new combinations will always emerge to startle and delight.

Parable (p. 91): *See Fable and Parable.*

Pathetic Fallacy (p. 87): This is the giving of human emotions to nature. When John Ruskin coined this term in 1856, perhaps he had something like this in mind: "The setting sun lovingly kissed the earth's cheek good night." Oy. However, let's say you have a young character in love for the first time. Her emotions cause her to see the world through a rosy lens; her love for Johnny is overflowing—she loves everybody and everything right now. The erroneous logic lies not in the author herself but is part of the protagonist's voice. Yet, were it to go on, ad nauseam, I suspect both would be critical targets. Since Ruskin, the term "pathetic fallacy" has been extended to include man-made objects as well. Don't fret; we all use the pathetic fallacy. It's just that when it succeeds, we call it by another name—metaphor.

Picaro/Picaresque Novel (p. 42): The Picaresque novel has been around since the 1500s and was in the making hundreds of years before that. *Don Quixote* by Cervantes is a well-known example. In this camp there's also Henry Fielding's *Tom Jones* and the wonderful *Moll Flanders* by Daniel Defoe. The picaro is a roaming rogue, and it's likely s/he may bump up against almost any type or class of person, and thus is ripe for social satire. From a bivouac to Kerouac, if the life of the carefree character on the road appeals to you, take good notes as you travel and let nothing escape your keen gaze. Don't expect to see the true picaro's character steadily evolve. Once a rouge . . .

Plot (p. 2): The fundamental difference between plot and story is that plot answers the question why. The implied causality has its roots in Aristotle's *Poetics*. While plot is like a main vein leading to the heart of a story, **subplot** is akin to a venule. Subordinate to the main plot line, it nonetheless adds color, dimension, and health to your story. Often a subplot or subplots tie into the main plot line before a story ends, but not always.

Point of View (p. 76): Though I've done the more traditional thing by divvying up point of view into various categories, missing is a discussion of distance and the techniques used to manipulate it. In addition to the person (first, third, etc.) I've illustrated, there's a question of distance between reader and character, narrator and character, author and character. (For starters, see Psychic Distance.) Check out any edition of Janet Burroway's *Writing Fiction*. See, too, Wayne C. Booth's classic *The Rhetoric of Fiction* and the chapter on point of view in David Jauss's book *On Writing Fiction.*

Premise (p. 50): If the world we enter is populated by fairies or talking spiders, orange water or green moons, the reader needs to believe that such things exist; that is, she must accept these ideas in order for the story to work. Sometimes readers are asked to make Kierkegaardian leaps of faith, and do so; other times, the reader, like the coyote, falls into the canyon and the author, as roadrunner, is all by himself. It's interesting to note that the same premise may succeed when written by one author and yet fail with another. Thinking about why this is so marks a fine place to begin pondering the topic.

Prologue (p. 65): This term comes from the Greek *"prologos"*: *"pro,"* "before," and *"logos,"* "discourse." Once upon a time, before the start of a play, an actor would come out onstage and give the audience background information. Since then writers of fiction have adopted and adapted the use of prologue at the beginning of a book often for the same reason the Greeks used a speaker before the beginning of a play. Additionally, in some genre forms, a prologue is used as a lure—you as reader are a gar on a barb, hooked for the duration of the book if the bait is tempting enough. Although a prologue can be considered an **introduction** of sorts, one often associates the word "introduction" with a composition or an explanatory essay (which could be about the author or the writing of the work itself). A nifty possibility to consider is what a prologue might allow the writer to do with point of view. A **preface** may also precede a work; sometimes it contains an **acknowledgment**—public recognition to those individuals or institutions that in some way had an impact on the work. As well, a preface may give the reader pertinent information about the story or the making of it. Henry James's prefaces were essays, themselves later collected into a book called *The Art of the Novel*. His hope was that these essays would become a manual of sorts for aspiring writers. They are painstakingly written and demand as much as they give. Often, a preface is dated. Both preface and **foreword** are frequently written by someone other than the author.

A prologue is a stylistic choice, and there should be a reason for it. Ask yourself if what you are writing could really go into Chapter 1 or perhaps more skillfully be embedded into the text as back story; if so, a prologue seems unnecessary.

Psychic Distance (p. 4): This is an intimacy issue between reader and character: the closer and more connected a reader feels, the less psychic distance; the less connection a reader feels toward a character, the greater the distance. It might be helpful to think of psychic distance as a continuum. At one end a reader may feel so connected as to *become* the character, and at the other extreme she may experience a distance so remote that the character seems as foreign to her as a creature from another galaxy. Along this continuum are as many possibilities as there are degrees of closeness in a relationship. Writers manipulate psychic distance for various effects. In the first example, narrative summary contributes to the distant tone. This is reinforced by a detached reportorial style and word choice. In the second example, the distance is less severe while in the last example, a scene unfolds. The mice are individuated. They are given names and dialogue, and the reader is privy to their thoughts and emotions, all of which can diminish the distance between reader and character.

Red Herring (p. 8): I think of this as a false scent. The reader sees and smells a fish, gets a good bit of detail about it, and as a result naturally expects it to play a part in the story, but it doesn't. An example that comes to mind is from *Tarzan of the Apes*, where the reader gets details about Tarzan learning French when this has absolutely nothing to do with the situation or story moment. A red herring is often a vestige of a previous draft. It's not only characters who can act as red herrings; anything that leads the reader astray and then vanishes—like a cheap plot device—can be considered a red herring.

Repetition (p. 64): The songwriter's refrain. The poet's alliterative line. The storyteller's use of three. The writer's anaphoric practice. All of these attest to the power of repetition in art and story form. But too much is too much, and unintended rhyme in midsentence can be deadly. Carefully chosen, repetition of words or phrases can aid in character development and story complexity. Study the rhythm in the prose of writers you admire and revisit some classic figures of speech. When was the last time you or your characters made use of "asyndeton" or "ploce" to turn a phrase?

Research (p. 82): While the mice and their unfolding story is fictional, in this chapter I've included factual tidbits about the origin and history of the rhyme of the "Three Blind Mice." Fiction doesn't mean that it's all made up; indeed, some master storytellers have achieved their status in part due to careful research and their ability to integrate historical facts and details into a story. Much of what a writer discovers in the course of research does not make it into the text proper nor should it, for the task is not to write an exhaustive treatise but to sift and incorporate those facts and details which are necessary to the telling of your story. Writers who can afford it often use research assistants. Harry "Rabbit" Angstrom in John Updike's famed series started out as a kitchen gadget salesman. When we catch up with Harry in a later sequel, he's inherited a Toyota dealership and the need to know, not only about cars and parts, but the nuts and bolts of running a dealership requires research. Writers have a natural curiosity about the world and their surroundings, and research will often take one on a wonderful, even surprising, journey. The possibility for serendipitous discoveries can unfold with the turning of the next page or thumbnail. The above holds true for stargazing futurists; successful writers of science fiction know their science facts.

Revision (p. 44): This is where the real fun and work begin. Often in the first draft we have no idea where we are going. We may overwrite, saturating the page in unnecessary detail; conversely, we may underwrite. We may call a character Harry on page one and Henry or Sam on page five. He may have a deadly allergy to peanuts on page three and on page fifteen, be munching a Snickers at the movies, but if we keep revising, eventually we'll get there. When interviewed by *The Paris Review*, the short-story czar Raymond Carver said he'd written as many as twenty or thirty drafts of a story and never less than ten or twelve. Virtually all writers revise, and some continue to do so long after the work has been published. For further wisdom and inspiration, take a look at Anne Lamott's "Shitty First Drafts" in *Bird by Bird*.

Roman à Clef (p. 95): Roughly translated, this French term *"roman"* ("novel") and *"clef"* ("key") refers to a book based on the disguised life (or lives) of public figures. Readers are "keyed," or "clued in," because of their familiarity with the real-life individuals. Because such novels are based on public figures, the interest is already primed (so too the possibility for lawsuits—resulting in higher sales). More than one writer has made her way to the bestseller list by "protesting too much" that her characters are not the actor X and the politician Y. Under the umbrella of fiction, writers have more room to shape a story. They can embellish or be satirical if it suits the telling. *Primary Colors* was originally published anonymously; no doubt the subject of the book was Bill Clinton and his presidential campaign. Almost all of Jack Kerouac's novels are of this type. Fitzgerald (*Tender Is the Night*) and Hemingway (*The Sun Also Rises*) wrote novels in this vein too.

Science Fiction (p. 113): Trying to define science fiction reminds me of *The Blind Men and the Elephant*, in which each blind man grabs hold of a different part of the elephant and declares he knows what an elephant is like. In the Snip of the Tale, I eliminate the word "future" because if time is an important part of the equation then conceivably, couldn't science fiction also embraces historical fiction? As a newer fictional form, I suspect both the term and genre will evolve and change over time. Here, though, is something few would dispute: A different world is not carte blanche for sloppy invention—if we're going to Mars, the writer must be familiar with the planet's terrain and salient facts.

Sentence Diagram (p. 59): The mice and I agree that no one can best Gertrude Stein when it comes to enthusiasm for diagramming sentences. To her nothing was more exciting than grammar and diagramming sentences when she was in school. In *Lectures in America* she extolls the "everlasting feeling of sentences as they diagram themselves. . . . In that way one is completely possessing something and incidentally one's self."

Sentimentality (p. 24): In fiction, sentimentality seeks to manipulate and exacerbate the reader's feelings by using a situation that, in and of itself, would trigger an emotional response, leaving by the wayside the reader's intellect. The same situation (for example, a character contemplating suicide), depending on its treatment, can drown us in emotion or lead us to reflect on the conditions that brought him to the bridge. Some readers may notice that the example given plays off the famous death scene of the saintly little Eva in *Uncle Tom's Cabin* by Harriet Beecher Stowe.

Setting (p. 23): In fiction, setting is defined simply as place and time. Conflict between characters and their setting advances the action and story line. In this scene on page 23, our sense of the mice as characters is deepened when we observe them in their personal environment. The setting is also used to reflect their emotional states. Effective setting helps establish the fictional world in the mind of the reader and contributes to the suspension of disbelief. If you have trouble with setting, try zeroing in on some significant descriptive details, or try thinking about it as a character—what is the room "wearing" for starters, what secrets is it privy to—and see if that helps you inject more life and energy into your surroundings.

Sex (p. 43): If you're squeamish about writing about sex, then you shouldn't. If all you want to write about is sex, there are plenty of outlets available for that. Somewhere in-between lies its treatment in contemporary fiction. If there's a reason for it in your story, then give sex the same care and attention as any other material before you. As Walt Whitman said, "The dirtiest book in all the world is the expurgated book."

Short Short Story (p. 105): How short can a short story be? Here's a well-known one attributed to Hemingway: "For sale: baby shoes, never worn." Short fiction is not new although many of the adjectives like "micro" and "flash" attempt to give it a modern facelift. Short fiction is defined in part by specific word length or range of words. If writing is a muscle, then exercising it in this short form will have you scrutinizing every word and its relation to the one next to it. It's harder than it seems.

Showing and Telling (p. 20): Like magicians, writers create their own kind of magic through years of reading, studying, and practicing. They learn that to show is an art and that attempting to tell the reader everything is like a magician explaining where the rabbit came from. There are times, however, when you do want to tell the reader something, and summarizing is a great and efficient way of doing just that. We learn as children that no one likes a "tattletale," but writers are all tattletales; the good ones get away with it because they know when to tell and when to keep their mouths shut and let the scene itself do the telling. I think of these two as separate, like salt and pepper, and yet they have complementary possibilities when used together.

Simile, Metaphor, and Conceit (p. 68): These are the knife, fork, and spoon that bring elegance to the literary feast. In general, simile is a form of comparison using "like" or "as," whereas metaphor is a direct comparison and thus can often wield a greater punch by virtue of compression. A conceit is an extended comparison that unfolds gradually, like a flower, and what the things compared have in common may not at first be obvious. A famous literary example of a conceit is John Donne's comparison of the Trinity to a flea.

Stereotype (p. 80): Stereotype is a form of cliché (see the entry on Cliché for origin of the term itself). In fiction, when we say that characters are stereotyped, we mean they are not individuated. To define all mice by their love of cheese is to ignore their complexity. Just like humans, their diets vary greatly. The house mouse will eat anything from Benadryl to peanut butter; other mice prefer seeds while still others include fruits and insects in their diet. Some mice do not drink water. Undoubtedly, mice, like humans, can carry disease. Imagine, however, human beings who were viewed only as vessels of disease. The historical consequences of such attitudes remain all too vivid.

Story (p. 1): This two-sentence example illustrates the concept that story is a sequence of narrative events. E. M. Forster discusses this notion at length in his classic *Aspects of the Novel*.

Stream of Consciousness (p. 15): Just think of this as a big pot of Irish stew—everything that happens to be around at the moment goes into the making of it, and thus becomes the food that feeds your character's consciousness. William James, psychologist and brother to Henry, picked up on this phrase in *The Principles of Psychology*. In the early twentieth century, as greater attention was given to the exploration of the unconscious mind, the psychological novel developed. It is in effect an endeavor to move beyond mere rational thought and to attempt to portray the total internal flow of experience. In stream-of-consciousness novels, one is often on a deep, nonverbal level, where the image must express what the words can't. But how does one capture thoughts and feelings that lack narrative sequence or logic? The publication of *Ulysses* by James Joyce was a groundbreaking example. Since we often do not think in complete sentences and quickly move from one thought to another, writers have tried various techniques to replicate this process on the page. Disjointed writing, omitting quotations, using fragments and words as symbols are all examples. You (and perhaps even your character) may well ask what a cardoon is doing in there? Next to a lotus root, no less—whatever could it mean? Slurp this: We sometimes have enough trouble figuring out what's brewing in our own stew, and being stuck too long in the dark borscht of a character's mind with no croutons to help us find our way out leads to pure stasis. I do think, with more nonlinear forms of writing that are beginning to emerge via computers, interesting treatments of the psychological novel may well emerge. Virginia Woolf, William Faulkner, James Joyce, Dorothy Richardson, and more recently Reinaldo Arenas all made use of stream of consciousness, or interior monologue, in their writing.

Structure (p. 103): There's a kind of freedom in structure. It offers a framework upon which you can begin to build your story. A ten-lira coin becomes the connecting device in Marguerite Yourcenar's *A Coin in Nine Hands*. Through it we travel around the city of

Rome in 1933 and gain entry into the lives of all who come into contact with it on a given day. Just as there are more structural considerations in building a high-rise than a hut, you'll need to plan accordingly if you want your book to stand up to the demands of the reader.

Style (p. 48): Developing one's style is like developing a sense of fashion. You may start off by trying on a lot of costume jewelry; big showy ten-dollar words. They'll get attention all right, but maybe you'll discover there's something better out there for you. Perhaps you'll try a charm bracelet full of dangling modifiers. Or a simple silver bracelet and an onyx ring. Keep experimenting for pleasant combinations, and a truer picture of yourself and your work will begin to emerge. So much of style is understanding what is yours as opposed to what is secondhand, and it takes time, so be patient. You must don and doff all manner of clothes in a quest for your own unique style. Look closely at others, and you will find even more combinations—some elaborate, some disconcerting. A pink shirt. Cufflinks made of teeth. Sometimes you may try to borrow the jewelry of others. Studded posts from Hemingway. Strands of tiny glass beads from Henry James. Pearls from Edith Wharton. A magnificent scarf from Homer that keeps unraveling. Embroidered shoes from Chaucer. A wand from J. K. Rowling. A hairshirt from Dostoyevsky. Many of us become writers because we have fallen in love with another writer's style and seek to emulate it. If you're going to pinch bits from others, you must learn to wear them as your own; that is, you must learn to *absorb* what those you admire have to teach you, not copy them.

It's really learning how to borrow the *essence* of their jewelry as opposed to the pieces themselves.

Subplot (p. 111): *See Plot.*

Suspense (p. 79): One can learn to create suspense just as one can learn to draw. It's a basic element. You study. You observe. You try. If you find yourself turning the pages even though you are tired and it is past your bedtime, look closely at what techniques the writer is using to keep you awake. Jot them down. Practice making them your own.

Suspension of Disbelief (p. 10): This term was coined in 1817 by Samuel Coleridge. Good fiction allows a reader to accept improbabilities; the reader suspends doubt and is pulled along in the story. In this case, blind mice playing poker. Like so much of successful writing, this is achieved by careful choice of detail. Buy your license early: in *The Hobbit*, notice how J. R. R. Tolkien *immediately* begins to convince us of the little peoples' existence.

Symbolism (p. 75): Symbols are everywhere. It's not surprising that they turn up in fiction, too. Many a high school student has endured a heavy-handed lecture on the symbolism in texts such as William Golding's *Lord of the Flies* or Arthur Miller's *The Crucible* almost to the exclusion of character. Symbols too can seem cliché after a while: the winter of death, the rebirth of spring, the tart in a red dress, the villain in a black hat. If you stay with your characters and situation, original and organic symbols are likely to emerge. Remember, you as writer are like a conductor. Let your characters play. Keep the ( ) at bay.

Tale (p. 104): Tales (including tall tales and folktales) have been around for ages. For various reasons, writers past and present have even yoked the term to their titles (*The Canterbury Tales, A Tale of Two Cities, The Handmaiden's Tale*). We have set ideas about how a short story should be constructed, perhaps more so with the rise and popularity of creative writing programs. "Tale" (true or fictitious) seems to be a broader term than "short story," which implies fiction. There's plenty of falsehood (and humor) in tall tales, which were part of the American frontier life. If you've never tried writing a tall tale, it's great fun. Perusing the work of Mark Twain and Bret Hart will energize and instruct you. For regional bawdy lore and humor, see Vance Randolph's *Pissing in the Snow and Other Ozark Folktales*.

Title (p. 26): Here, the mice bicker over what constitutes an effective title, and understandably so, for a myriad of possibilities and considerations exist. If you are having trouble coming up with a title for your own work, it may be an indication that perhaps you are unsure where you are going, or perhaps unclear what your story is really about. Keep writing, as the process is likely to clarify this for you. I think it helps to have a working title—even if it's one you're sure to reject. Living with and then eliminating a title that "isn't right" brings you closer to one that is. An interesting historical tidbit: It wasn't uncommon for some early titles to be longer than today's microfictions.

About this Title: *Thrice Told Tales* has numerous meanings, the most obvious being the play on tails—referring to both story and mice—and three being the number of mice as well as a number suggesting repetition, and rightly so, for the same story is either continually referenced or retold. It also has roots in folklore and literature, three being a number Alan Dundes exhaustively researched in fairy tales; he said of American culture: "The child is conditioned by his folklore to expect three and his culture does not disappoint him." But the title is also a reference to Nathaniel Hawthorne's *Twice-Told Tales*, a collected series of sketches and tales first published individually in various periodicals, then later collected and reprinted (thus "twice-told"). In his 1842 review of Hawthorne's book, Edgar Allen Poe wrote: "The book professes to be a collection of *tales*, yet is, in two respects, misnamed. These pieces are now in their third republication, and, of course, are thrice-told. Moreover, they are by no means all tales, either in the ordinary or in the legitimate understanding of the term."

Tour de Force (p. 117): This refers to a true show of skill. See Raymond Queneau's *Exercises in Style* or Art Spiegelman's *Maus*.

Tragedy (p. 115): Over the ages, this term has had many meanings. Classically, it is the toppling of an individual due to circumstance or some inner flaw. Once tragic figures were imperfect heroes and gods. Queens and kings. By the 1700s the middle class became subjects of tragedy. How a character handles misfortune is often at the heart of modern fiction. Like horror, tragedy is what we all want to watch with our windows safely rolled up at a drive-in theater (see Catharsis), yet we all learn about tragedy by reading the newspaper, watching the telly, and—ultimately—in the course of living our own lives.

Transitions (p. 28): Onstage, transition is easy: a curtain comes down. Or the actors freeze momentarily—known as a tableau—to signal an end or a shift. Often the lighting is dimmed and stage rats rearrange the furniture to create a new setting. But the writer has no behind-the-scenes crew to assist her. She must get her characters from one place or time to another on her own. So how does a writer create smooth transitions? A good transition is like a good transmission—it aids in a smooth ride. When it's properly functioning, you don't even think about it as you're zipping along, enjoying the scenery and anticipating what's up ahead. If it starts to slip, it's harder for you to go forward with the same speed and pleasure. As a writer, you've got to be more than just a good mechanic, you've got to also be able to fine-tune transitions so that your story remains fluid. Use too much white space on the page, and your reader will feel that she is in a blizzard, drained of all her energy and unable to find her way to the end of the story.

Whiteout aside, using weather gets the job done. Seasons connote longer time lapses; weather itself is more immediate, yet both illustrate the passage of time and in this sense are natural transitions. So, too, is time itself. Almost all objects can be used to indicate the passage of time and therefore function as transitions: new shoes to worn heels; marshmallows melting in hot chocolate; rust on a car. Mary's sagging mammae.

The riddle of the sphinx reminds us of the changing human form over time. Perceptive writers use appearance to create transition from one time to another: from clean shaven to five o'clock shadow; from stubble to goatee; from ringlets to payis that touch the tallit. Daily activities also help the writer form transitions: a shower, a game of basketball, watching a TV program, the ending of a live eBay auction. Try also to involve the reader in your transition by signaling its approach. She will be anything but lost (and she may well feel a bit smug anticipating what's up ahead).

In addition to transitions related to time and space, there's a more daunting challenge of creating fluid transitions in and out of various points of view. Never underestimate the power of a name in getting you there.

Translation (p. 46): We humans sometimes have enough trouble understanding one another when we speak the same language. If you've ever played the childhood game of telephone—where one person whispers something into her neighbor's ear and it's whispered ear to ear down the line, with the last person speaking the words aloud—then you're familiar with the uproarious results that often have nothing to do with the original utterance. It doesn't take much to imagine the problems posed by translating a major work into another language. More and more, writers—especially poets—are beginning to pair up and team-translate in a time when ideas of individual authorship and ownership are called into question. Many look toward the machine as a translation tool. You may want to try your hand at translating something of yours into another language. There's nothing like learning the grammar of another language to teach you the grammar of your own. Altavista's Babelfish gives a rough translation (what some call gisting). A suave pickup line outside its native language might sound like this: Me Tarzan. You Jane. Come tree house. Drink coconut. Have swinging time. Me chest pound and yodel you.

There are software tools that aid the translator, but so far no Hal or R2-D2 has been invented that can do it all, and so for now we rely on one another as we have since the fall of Babble. For translation woes and commentary, check out Mark Twain's "The Celebrated Jumping Frog of Calaveras County." This amusing story was so poorly translated into French—Twain said, "I think it is the worst I ever saw; and yet the French are called a polished nation"—that Twain felt compelled to retranslate the French version.

Unreliable Narrator (p. 66): In *Writing Fiction*, Janet Burroway has astute things to say about narrative craft, including the unreliable narrator. The unreliable narrator has limitations that we as readers generally do not share. These limitations may be experiential (age related), emotional, or psychological (grief over the sudden loss of a loved one, pathological lying). Limitations may be due to hereditary (deafness) or environmental factors (characters placed in an alien setting), or they may be chemically induced (drugs, alcohol). Because of their limitations, unreliable narrators are not to be trusted. As a writer you must clue your reader early on that your narrator is unreliable. Skillful writers are purposeful in their use of unreliable narrators. Bone (the young narrator in Dorothy Allison's *Bastard Out of Carolina*) lacks the vocabulary and experience to articulate and understand that her stepfather is sexually abusing her. All she knows is that it doesn't feel good. The reader, however, understands exactly what is happening. To use or not to use an unreliable narrator depends on the story you want to tell and how you want to tell it. While you're ruminating you might want to take a look at *Notes from Underground* by Fyodor Dostoyevsky, *Aztec* by Gary Jennings, or *The Sound and the Fury* by William Faulkner.

Verisimilitude (p. 98): This is the likeness to truth, the quality of seeming true. Verisimilitude is also at play when a writer blends bizarre and fantastical facts into a story so that they appear true. Stephen King is a master of this. Read him. And for inspiration and good solid advice, check out his book *On Writing: A Memoir of the Craft*. The conversational style of it will pull you along and make you sad to reach the end.

Vocabulary and Syntax (p. 18): Mark Twain said, "The difference between the almost right word and the right word is really a large matter—'tis the difference between the lightning-bug and the lightning." The hunt for the right word might mean much time spent on one sentence. That should never be considered a waste of time; rather, a reminder that on such days you know you are doing your job, for who else would take such care with language? Don't be seduced by big words alone. Learn as many four letter words as you can. To paraphrase Hemingway, if a writer insists on putting something in the work for its own sake (say, to showcase the knowledge of the writer), the whole work suffers.